Cultivating Stillness

清靜經

Cultivating Stillness

A TAOIST MANUAL FOR TRANSFORMING BODY AND MIND

With a commentary by Shui-ch'ing Tzu
Translated with an introduction
BY *EVA WONG*
Illustrations by Hun-yen Tzu

SHAMBHALA
Boston & London
1992

Shambhala Publications, Inc.
Horticultural Hall
300 Massachusetts Avenue
Boston, Massachusetts 02115
www.shambhala.com

18 17 16 15 14 13 12 11

Printed in the United States of America
♾ This edition is printed on acid-free paper that meets the
American National Standards Institute z39.48 Standard.
♻ Shambhala Publications makes every effort to print on recycled paper.
For more information please visit www.shambhala.com.

Distributed in the United States by Random House, Inc.,
and in Canada by Random House of Canada Ltd

Library of Congress Cataloging-in-Publication Data

Ch'ing ching ching t'u. English.
Cultivating stillness, with an illustrated commentary: a Taoist manual for transforming body and mind/translated and with an introduction by Eva Wong.—1st ed.
p. cm.
ISBN 978-0-87773-687-5 (pbk.: alk. paper)
1. Ch'ing ching ching—Commentaries. I. Wong, Eva, 1951–
II. Title.
BL1900.C41513 1992 92-50120
299'.51444—dc20 CIP

Contents

Translator's Introduction

I made my first exploration of the Taoist canon when I was fourteen years old. I was living in Hong Kong then, and I was studying the *Tao-te Ching* (also known as the *Lao-tzu)* and the *Chuang-tzu* in a Chinese literature course in high school. I developed an instant liking for the philosophy in these two texts, but during that time I had no idea of the vastness of the Taoist canon. For the rest of the school year I ignored all the other materials in the course and studied only these two books. This almost ended in disaster because the *Lao-tzu* and the *Chuang-tzu* comprised only one-tenth of the required textual material in the course. However, during that period I also discovered the less known sections of the Taoist canon. In my search for commentaries related to these two books I ran into the section of the canon that contained the commentaries on the *Chuang-tzu,* known as the *Chuang-tzu Nan-h'ua P'ien,* and the "apocryphal" writings of Lao-tzu. The latter included texts such as the *T'ai Shang Hua-hu Ching,* the *T'ai Shang Kan-ying P'ien,* and the *T'ai Shang Ch'ing-ching Ching (Cultivating Stillness).* I passed the course by sheer luck. That year, the examination questions emphasized Taoist philosophy, and my research into materials beyond the course requirement balanced my ignorance of all the other areas of Chinese literature.

Between my regular school activities I squeezed in a few hours each week to study the Taoist texts. A year later I started learning *feng-shui,* or Chinese geomancy, from my granduncle. Feeling the similarity between Taoism and feng-shui, I asked my granduncle about the Taoist texts that I had been studying. By then I already had two commentaries on *Cultivating Stillness* and had just found the *Huang-t'ing Ching* (the *Yellow Palace Classic*). My granduncle replied that *Cultivating Stillness* and its commentaries were part of an esoteric tradition of Taoism known as internal alchemy (that is, the transformation of body and mind toward health and longevity). He also told me that I was venturing into an area in which understanding of the texts required guidance from a Taoist master.

I was unable to find a Taoist master until many years later. Ironically, it was not in Hong Kong but in the United States that I found my master. When I first met Mr. Moy Lin-shin, I knew he was the teacher I was looking for, although he did not "look" like a Taoist master I had imagined. In fact, he never claimed to be one. When I started studying with him, my teacher *(si-fu)* did not talk about Taoism, let alone internal alchemy. Even after I was initiated into the Taoist temple he cofounded, most of what he taught me were techniques of "tendon-changing" and *t'ai-chi* and *i-ch'uan* instructions for improving my health. It was only when I showed signs of "external tempering" of the body that he began to tell me to cultivate stillness of mind. He told me that by dissolving desire through helping others, I would "tame" my mind and reach the next level of training. At the same time he started giving me formal instructions in meditation.

Looking back on his actions, I now realize that my si-fu's approach came from the Northern School of Taoism. The Northern School recommended cultivating the body before cultivating the mind. In contrast, the Southern School focused on cultivation of the mind first, and then cultivation of the body. The Northern School is represented by the Lungmen sect of Complete Reality Taoism and the various sects of the Huashan system, including the Hsien-t'ien (Earlier Heaven) Wu-chi sect. Later, I discovered that the lineage of my si-fu's temple, the one that I had been initiated into, descended from the Earlier Heaven Wu-chi sect.

It was six years after my initiation into the temple when my si-fu started to talk about internal alchemy and steered me toward the texts of the Taoist canon. When I mentioned that I had been studying the canon texts he did not seem surprised. His comment was simply: "That's good."

In the summer of 1987 I assisted my si-fu in a seminar on Taoism. He handed me a book and said casually, "Read over these chapters and talk about them tomorrow." The book he handed me was *Cultivating Stillness: With an Illustrated Commentary*. After the seminar, he told me that this text was used in many Taoist temples' introductory curriculum for initiates, and that I should someday make it available to the non-Chinese-reading community.

Three years passed before I felt I was ready to translate the text and the accompanying commentary. During this time, my si-fu explained the inner teachings of the text to me and taught me the methods of internal transformation discussed in the text and the commentary. The text came alive and I no longer felt like a "reader" of a book but a participant in the unfolding of a sequence of internal events in myself.

Historical Background

Cultivating Stillness is a text from the Taoist canon. Its Chinese name is the *T'ai Shang Ch'ing-ching Ching* (太上清靜經). The name attributes its authorship to T'ai Shang Lao-chun, a title given to Lao-tzu within the Taoist religion. The Taoist canon includes several works that are attributed to Lao-tzu but were not written by the historical Lao-tzu. Some of these were written by anonymous authors whose perspectives on Taoism resembled most closely the philosophical Taoism expressed in the *Tao-te Ching*. Others were written by authors who wanted to show that internal alchemy traced its spiritual origins to the philosophy in the *Lao-tzu*. *Cultivating Stillness* belongs to the latter group of texts.

Cultivating Stillness itself is a short text of twenty-four segments. It is believed to be written in the Six Dynasties Era (220–589 C.E.) although it was written in the literary form of the Warring States Period (475–221 B.C.E.). This was probably to highlight its philosophical closeness to the *Tao-te Ching*. A number of ideas expressed in *Cultivating Stillness* show strong influence of internal alchemy characteristic of the Eastern Han Period (25–220 C.E.). These are most prominent in chapters 1, 2, 3, 4, 9, and 16.

Cultivating Stillness, however, differed from the early alchemical texts in one important aspect. The early texts of internal alchemy written during the Eastern Han and the Chin dynasties (265–420 C.E.), like the *Triplex Unity* and the writings of Ko Hung, did not attempt to show that the arts of longevity and immortality were the logical development of the philosophy presented in the *Tao-teh Ching*. The philosophical approach in *Cultivating Stillness* shows the maturity of the internal alchemical school. The text skillfully blends classical Taoism and alchemical Taoism to convey multiple levels of interpretation. An exoteric (or literal) interpretation will produce a reading of Taoism that focuses on the ideas of *wu-wei,* simplicity, and peaceful and harmonious living. An esoteric interpretation will reveal hidden instructions on internal alchemy and meditation, and will offer advice on a lifestyle that is conducive to the cultivation of health and longevity.

Commentaries on *Cultivating Stillness* were written in the Five Dynasties Era (907–960 C.E.), the Southern Sung dynasty (1127–1279 C.E.), the Chin dynasty of the Manchus (1115–1234 C.E.), the Yüan dynasty (1271–1368 C.E.), the Ming dynasty (1368–1644 C.E.), and the Ch'ing dynasty (1644–1911 C.E.). The illustrated commentary in this translation contains the least esoteric terminology and was probably intended for novice initiates rather than advanced adepts. The author of the commentary was named Shui-ch'ing Tzu and the illustrations were by Hun-yen Tzu. These names are pseudonyms. As is true of many authors of the texts of the canon, little is known about their lives.

The literary style and the ideas expressed in the commentary place its authorship no earlier than the latter part of the Ming dynasty (1628–1644 C.E.). In fact, several aspects of the commentary and illustrations suggest that they were products of the Ch'ing dynasty (1644–1911 C.E.). First, there are references to Ming dynasty works. For example, the references to the Monkey King and the Pig Immortal show the author's familiarity with the Ming dynasty novel *Journey to the West.* Second, the ease with which the commentary's author blends Taoism, Buddhism, and Confucianism shows influence of the synthesis of the three philosophies popular during the late Ming period. Finally, historical records suggest that canonical texts that attempt to synthesize the three religions of China did not begin to appear in large numbers until the late Ming and early Ch'ing dynasties.

This translation is made from an edition of the text and the illustrated commentary printed in the Ch'ing dynasty. The printer's seal on the book says that it was reprinted in the eleventh year of the reign of Tung Chih in the Ch'ing dynasty (1873). Although we do not know how many printings the book went through, it can be reasonably assumed that the book enjoyed enough popularity to warrant repeated printings.

Philosophical Background

Taoist methods of health, longevity, and immortality were often presented in the esoteric terminology of alchemy, which was intended both to reveal and to hide. To those initiated in the practice, the symbolism revealed a world of inner experience. To the uninitiated, the terminology would appear confusing if not meaningless.

The Taoist methods of longevity involve powerful procedures of working with the body's internal energy. Without proper guidance from a qualified teacher, the methods can harm the practitioner. In addition, the methods of gathering, storing, purifying, and circulating internal energy can be abused by people whose minds are not clear of desire. Thus, from its beginnings, the transmission of the techniques of internal alchemy was exclusively through oral tradition. Any written material was considered as supplementary notes. These notes were either insights on existing teachings, new theoretical perspectives, or developments in methods and techniques.

As the Taoist arts of health and longevity became popular, writings on these topics multiplied. Many of them were written by people whose familiarity with these techniques was limited to hearsay or acquaintance with some of the early, well-known works of internal alchemy such as the *Triplex*

Unity (*Tsan-tung Chi*), the *Yellow Palace Classic* (*Huang-t'ing Ching*), or the *Yellow Emperor's Classic of the Convergence of Yin* (*Huang-ti Yin-fu Ching*). The fascination with internal alchemy and the popularity of the arts of longevity led many writers to use the jargon of esoteric symbolism to gain credibility for their works. This resulted in texts that contain much esoteric terminology and little substance. The degeneration of Taoist internal alchemy was at its worst during the late T'ang dynasty (618–906 C.E.) and the Era of the Five and Ten Kingdoms (907–960 C.E.). The fad at the time was to see who could come up with the most esoteric rendition of the Taoist theory and practice.

By the time of the Sung (960–1279 C.E.) and Ming dynasties, there were strong reactions against esoteric symbolism in Taoist writing. Movement toward a simpler and more direct way of presenting Taoist theory and practice emerged. Both the Northern and Southern branches of the Complete Reality School and the Huashan School of Chen Hsi-i attempted to "demythologize" Taoist internal alchemy. The writings from these schools contained less alchemical symbolism. Their approach differed from both the Han dynasty (206 B.C.E.–219 C.E.) and the T'ang dynasty works. In the Han texts, internal alchemy was almost synonymous with the cultivation of the body (for example see the *Triplex Unity* and the writings of Ko Hung). In the T'ang texts there was considerable confusion over what the technical terminology of internal alchemy referred to. However, in the Sung dynasty, Taoist internal alchemy emphasized the dual cultivation of body and mind, and clearing the mind of desire was increasingly viewed as complementary to the cultivation of physical health.

In the Ch'ing dynasty, textual analysis became a major activity in Chinese literature. It was during this time that many commentaries and critical evaluations of the Taoist texts were written. Some commentaries attempted to "demystify" the Taoist texts, arguing that the symbolic language was simply gibberish, and that the esoteric language functioned merely to surround Taoism with an aura of mystery. These commentaries sought to "psychologize" internal alchemy, asserting that the processes of internal alchemy can be explained as mental phenomena. Others saw meaning in the symbolism, but felt that without clarification by commentaries, the true meaning of the text would remain hidden. These commentators sought to "demythologize" the texts, but were careful to point out that the commentaries were not meant to be "stand-alone" manuals, and that the reader should seek guidance from a qualified teacher.

Cultivating Stillness was written in the Six Dynasties Era, before alchemical symbolism was abused. This is evident in its scant use of internal alchemy's technical terminology. The author's intention was to show that the spiritual origin of the arts of longevity lay in the philosophy of Lao-tzu. The illustrated commentary that accompanied this edition of *Cultivating Stillness* was written after the scholarly reaction against the abuse of alchemical symbolism. Although the commentary was intended to reveal hidden meanings of alchemical Taoism, the need to receive proper instruction from a teacher was emphasized throughout the book. In this way, *Cultivating Stillness* and its illustrated commentary resembled the spirit of the early teachings of the arts of longevity. The book was meant as a supplement to an oral tradition.

Major Ideas of Taoist Internal Alchemy

TAOIST COSMOLOGY AND INTERNAL ALCHEMY

Taoist cosmology and internal alchemy are best illustrated by Chen Hsi-i's *wu-chi* diagram, and much of the commentary of *Cultivating Stillness* assumes familiarity with this diagram. In particular, the wu-chi diagram served as the basis of ideas on the origin and creation of things discussed in chapters 1, 2, 3, and 4.

According to the *Chronicles of Huashan (Huashan chi)* the wu-chi diagram was carved on a cliff face in Huashan, the Grand Mountains of the Shensi province. It is said that the wu-chi diagram was first revealed to a Taoist hermit known as the Sage of the River who passed it on to Wei Po-yang, author of the *Triplex Unity*. Chung Li-ch'uan, one of the Eight Immortals, obtained the knowledge of the wu-chi diagram and transmitted it to Lü Tung-pin. Lü lived as a hermit on Huashan and passed the teachings on to Chen Hsi-i. Chen Hsi-i was a Sung dynasty Taoist hermit who resided on Huashan. He was reputed to have originated unique forms of sleeping postures of *chi-kung,* the internal martial art form known as *Hsin-I Liu He Pa Fa Ch'uan* (the Six Harmonies and Eight Methods Form), the celestial divination system *Tzu-wei Tu-su,* and to have written various treatises on Taoist cosmology and internal alchemy.

The wu-chi diagram describes the Taoist theory of the universe as well as the process of cultivating the internal pill. The internal pill is the culmination of gathering, purifying, and storing of internal energy in the body. It is the seed of the spirit god *(yüan-shen)* and the essence of health and longevity.

The concept of wu-ch'i is uniquely Taoist. Its usage can be traced back to chapter 28 of the *Lao-tzu,* which first mentions "the return to the wu-ch'i." The *Chuang-tzu* also says "enter the Nameless Gate" and "wander in the expanse of wu-chi." Wu-chi is the Taoist conception of the origin or source of all things. On the other hand, the concept of t'ai-chi comes from Confucianism. It was first mentioned in the *I Ching,* a Confucianist classic: "from t'ai-chi comes the two oppo-

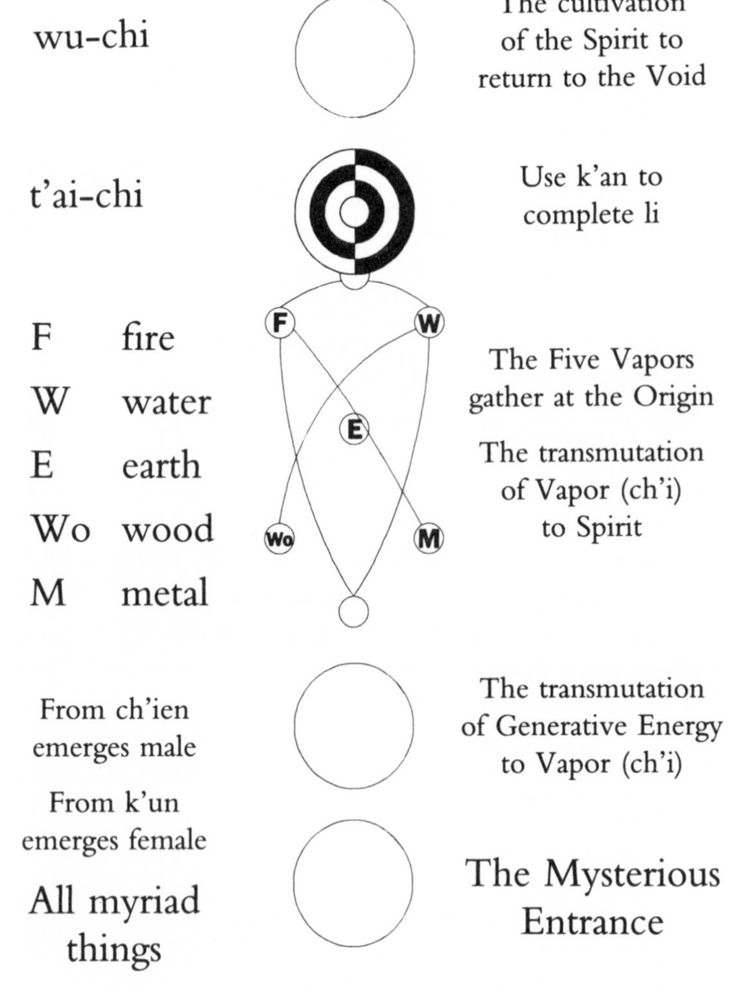
wu-chi
The cultivation
of the Spirit to
return to the Void
t'ai-chi
Use k'an to
complete li
F fire
W water
E earth
Wo wood
M metal
F
W
E
Wo
M
The Five Vapors
gather at the Origin
The transmutation
of Vapor (ch'i)
to Spirit
From ch'ien
emerges male
From k'un
emerges female
All myriad
things
The transmutation
of Generative Energy
to Vapor (ch'i)
The Mysterious
Entrance

Figure 1.

The wu-chi diagram.

sites." T'ai-chi is the Confucianist conception of the source of all things.

The wu-chi diagram can be read from the top down or from the bottom up. Read from the top down, the diagram describes the origin of the universe and life. Read from the bottom up it describes the sequence of transformations in internal alchemy.

The Taoist origin of the universe and life is expounded by Chu-hsi of the Sung dynasty (960–1279 C.E.), who combined the Confucianist and Taoist theories of the origin of things. He revised Chou Tuan-i's treatise *T'ai-chi T'ao Shuo* and wrote, "From wu-chi comes t'ai-chi. When t'ai-chi moves, it creates yang. When movement reaches its extreme, stillness emerges. In stillness, yin is born. Thus, movement and stillness follow each other. Yin and yang, stillness and movement form the force of creation. From yang and yin are created the elements water, fire, wood, metal, and earth. The Five Vapors mutually enrich each other and generate the four seasons. The five elements originate from yin and yang. Yin and yang originate from t'ai-chi and t'ai-chi originates from wu-chi. From the properties of the five elements and the essence of wu-chi emerges generative energy. From the Way of Heaven *(ch'ien),* male is born. Following the Way of Earth *(k'un),* female is born. The union of ch'ien and k'un gives rise to the ten thousand myriad things. The ten thousand myriad things procreate and contribute to many forms of existence whose origin is wu-chi." This is the description of the origin of things.

Read from the bottom up, the wu-chi diagram describes the process of transformation through internal alchemy, or the return to the Tao. The circle at the bottom is the Mysterious Gate, or the Valley Spirit. *Gate* means "opening," and *Valley* refers to "Emptiness" or "Void." On the physical level the Valley Spirit lies in the Life Gate *(ming-men)* on the spinal column (an area on the spine between the kidneys). The ming-men controls movement of generative energy in the lower *tan-t'ien* (the area near the navel). On the spiritual level, the Valley Spirit is consciousness emptied of sensations, emotions, and thoughts.

The process of raising energy to the circle above it is known as the Transmutation of Generative Energy into Vapor *(ch'i)*. During the alchemical process, generative energy, which has form, is purified and transformed into a less tangible form of energy known as vapor. Continuing upward in the diagram, the next process is the Transmutation of Vapor into Spiritual Energy, or *ling-ch'i*. The mundane breath is transformed into Spiritual Energy. Ling-ch'i is formless and can be channelled to the internal organs and all parts of the body. When the body is filled with this energy, the state is known as the Five Vapors Gathering at the Origin.

The next stage of the process is illustrated by the concentric circles with interleaving black and white semicircles. This is the early rendition of the t'ai-chi symbol. In this stage, *k'an* (water) and *li* (fire) interact. This is the "immersion of fire in water." The spirit god (yüan-shen) is conceived and born, bringing the alchemical process to completion. This is the wu-chi, the circle at the top, which is the Origin, the Source, or the Tao. This final stage is known as the cultivation of the spirit god to return to the Void.

TAOIST INTERNAL ALCHEMY AND THE I CHING

The use of *I Ching* symbols is central to Taoist internal alchemy. Primary among these is the *pa-k'ua*. The pa-k'ua of Earlier Heaven is from the *Ho-to* and the pa-k'ua of Later Heaven comes from the *Lo-shu*. The Ho-to (the Pattern from the River) was a pattern inscribed on a horse that emerged from the floods of a river to reveal itself to the ancient emperor and sage Fu-hsi. The Lo-shu (the Book from the River Lo) was a pattern inscribed on the shell of a tortoise that came out of the waters of the River Lo to reveal itself to the Emperor Yu. Both patterns form the philosophical foundation of the *I Ching*.

The pa-k'ua of Earlier Heaven describes an ideal state of existence, when everything is in harmony and connected to the Tao. The Later Heaven pa-k'ua describes the state of existence which is not so perfect and not so harmonious. The return to the Tao (the path of longevity and immortality) refers to the transformation of our Later Heaven existence to that of Earlier Heaven and the recovery of our original nature. These ideas are discussed in chapters 19, 20, and 21 of *Cultivating Stillness*. The description of internal alchemy as the transformation of the Later Heaven pa-k'ua into the Earlier Heaven pa-k'ua is central to the teachings of the Earlier Heaven Wu-chi sect of the Huashan school.

The *Tsan-tung Chi* is one of the earliest works of internal alchemy to use symbolism from the *I Ching* to describe the process of internal alchemy and the cyclical movement of internal energy in the body. In this classic of internal alchemy, the process of returning to the Tao is described as "placing ch'ien and k'un in their positions" and letting k'an and li interact so that the yang element in k'an changes place with the yin element in li. Solid lines in trigrams symbolize yang while broken lines symbolize yin. Ch'ien and k'un represent heaven and earth in the Earlier Heaven pa-k'ua. K'an and li represent water and fire in the Later Heaven pa-k'ua. Ch'ien is pure yang and is symbolized by three solid lines (☰). K'un is pure yin and is symbolized by three broken lines (☷). When the solid line in k'an is taken to replace the broken line in li (☲), and the broken line in li is taken to replace the solid line in k'an (☵), the process is known as filling li with k'an. When the exchange of the yang and yin elements in

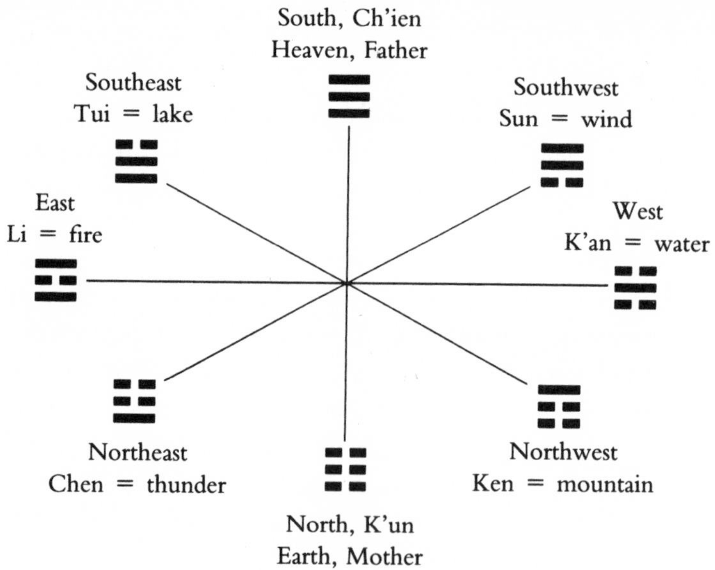

Earlier Heaven pa-k'ua

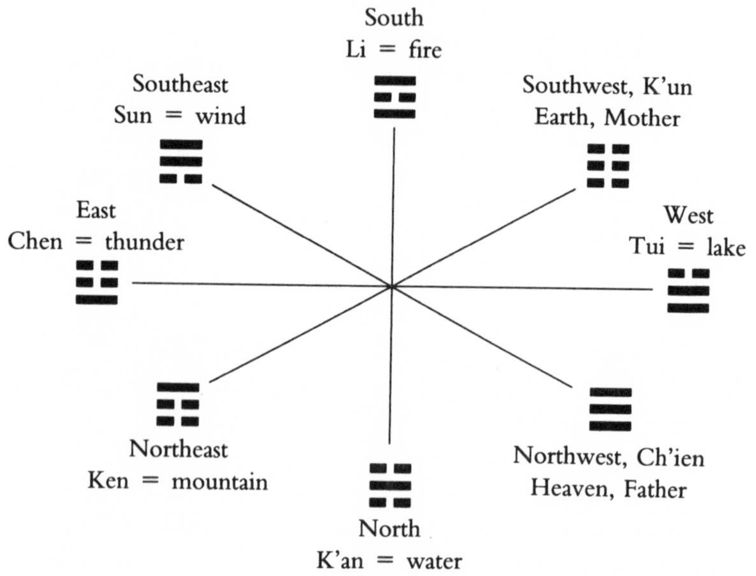

Later Heaven pa-k'ua

Figure 2.

The Earlier Heaven and Later Heaven pa-k'ua.

k'an and li is completed, there are only three solid lines and three broken lines, ch'ien and k'un. The complete transformation of the Later Heaven pa-k'ua into the Earlier Heaven pa-k'ua is discussed in detail in chapter 21.

In Taoist internal alchemy, health and longevity are also described in terms of the waxing and waning of yang and yin. These ideas are discussed in chapters 9 and 16. In this context, the hexagrams of the *I Ching* take on meanings different from their usage in divination. The alchemical meanings of the hexagrams are discussed in various commentaries of the *Tsan-tung Chi* and the *I-tao Hsin-fa* (translated by Thomas Cleary respectively as *The Taoist I Ching* and *I Ching Mandalas*, both published by Shambhala Publications).

In the illustrated commentary of *Cultivating Stillness*, *fu* (䷗), *lin* (䷒), *t'ai* (䷊), *chuang* (䷡), *kuai* (䷪), and *ch'ien* (䷀) are hexagrams in which yang is waxing, or rising. The waxing of yang is indicated in the hexagram by the presence of the solid lines in the lower portion of the hexagram. These symbolize growth and the gathering of internal energy. Thus, fu is first yang and lin is second yang, and so on. *K'ou* (䷫), *tun* (䷠), *pi* (䷋), *kuan* (䷓), *po* (䷖), and *k'un* (䷁) are hexagrams in which yang is waning, or dying. The waxing of yin is depicted in the hexagram by the presence of the broken lines in the lower portion of the hexagram. These hexagrams symbolize aging and the loss of internal energy. Therefore, k'ou is first yin and tun is second yin, and so on. Ch'ien is yang at its zenith and k'un is yin at its height. The rise of yang and yin is illustrated by the progressive dominance of the solid (yang) and broken (yin) lines in the hexagrams. In their waxing and waning, yang and yin both rise from the bottom of the hexagram. It is as if in the rise of yang, the alchemical foundations are built from the ground up, and in the rise of yin, it is the foundation that is eroded first.

THE CULTIVATION OF INTERNAL ENERGY AS AN ALCHEMICAL PROCESS

In Taoism, the attainment of health and longevity is likened to the tempering and refining of base metals into pure metal. Therefore, analogies such as pumping the bellows, tempering the sword, heating the cauldron, and kindling the stove have been used to describe the alchemical process. All these expressions are associated with refining and purifying the body. The refined body is often called the golden body.

THE THREE TREASURES.

The three treasures are also known as the three flowers, the three jewels, or the three herbs. They are *ching* (generative energy), *ch'i* (vital energy or vapor) and *shen* (spiritual energy, or ling-ch'i). These three energies were originally uncontaminated when we were in our mother's womb. In their pure form they are "original generative energy," "original vapor," and "original spirit." When we breathe earthly air, engage in sexual activity, think and become attached to things in the world, ch'i, ching, and shen become impure, thus losing their Earlier Heaven quality. The aim of the internal alchemical process is to gather and recover these three energies, refine them, and transform them to the original state. The process of refinement is labeled the gathering of the three flowers (or herbs) in the cauldron, the cauldron being the crucible where the refinement takes place.

THE STOVE AND THE CAULDRON.

The stove is the generator and the cauldron is the crucible where the refinement of the three energies takes place. In the purification of the three treasures, the lower tan-t'ien is the stove. This is where the alchemical fire is formed. Ching, ch'i, and shen are purified respectively in the three cauldrons—the lower, middle, and upper tan-t'ien. In the physical body, upper tan-t'ien is centered between the eyebrows, the middle tan-t'ien is centered at the solar plexus, and the lower tan-t'ien is centered one inch below the navel. The tan-t'ien is not a point (as in a chakra) but an area, as denoted by the word *t'ien,* meaning "field."

THE MICROCOSMIC CIRCULATION.

This is the pathway through which the internal energy circulates in the body. The circuit runs through two meridians in the body, the *tu* meridian and the *jen* meridian. The tu meridian starts at the base of the spine, and runs up the spine through the neck, up into the head, and descends down the front of the head through the crown to between the eyebrows. From there it descends to the palate where it ends. Structurally, the jen meridian starts at the navel. In one direction it ascends the front of the body and ends at the palate where it joins the tu meridian. In the other direction it descends from the navel and goes through the sperm palace (in males) or the ovarian palace (in females) and ends in the perineum. The Microcosmic Circulation is also known as the Lesser Achievement.

When the blockages in the tu and jen meridians are opened, they form a connected pathway and the internal energy can flow in a circulatory motion. The tan-t'ien in the abdomen will be connected to the crown of the head. Since the abdominal area is symbolized by yin and the crown of the head is symbolized by yang, the consequence of connecting the tu and jen meridians is the meeting of the water of k'an in the abdomen with the fire of li in the head. This is the meeting of k'an and li, the immersion of fire in water, resulting in the recovery of ch'ien and k'un. It is also called the turning of the waterwheel, or returning the ching to the brain.

When the three energies circulate through the entirety of the body, going from head to foot, the Macrocosmic Circulation is achieved. This is also known as the Greater Achievement, or the Descent of the Three True Fires to the Bubbling Spring.

The Stages in the Return to the Tao are as follows.

1. The refinement (or purification) of ching for transmutation of ch'i;
2. The refinement (or purification) of ch'i for transmutation of shen;
3. The cultivation of shen to return to the Void (or emptiness);
4. The cultivation of the Void to merge with the Tao.

The Six Stages of the Firing Process are as follows.

1. *The birth of yang.* This marks the initial appearance of yang, or the life force. In internal alchemy it refers to the starting of the fires of the stove. Only when the lower tan-t'ien becomes a generator can the three cauldrons be heated. Other descriptions of this stage are tempering the sword, kindling the fires, tempering the self, and strengthening the foundations. The stove is often referred to as the foundation since it is the energy source that makes the refining of the three energies possible.

2. *The emergence of the herbs.* The herbs are purified ching, ch'i, and shen. This stage marks the emergence of the three flowers or treasures in their refined form. The process involves gathering ching and refining it in the lower tan-t'ien for the transmutation of the gross ch'i into purified ch'i. When breath descending to the lower tan-t'ien is met by purified ching rising, a vapor is formed. This vapor is ch'i, or purified vital energy. The process is called the "immersion of

fire in water," where water symbolizes ching and fire symbolizes breath. When purified ching (water) is preserved in the body, it will rise. When purified breath (fire) is controlled, it will sink. When sexual cravings are dissolved, generative energy will not be dissipated. When the heart is empty of craving and anger, the fire will be in control and the flames will sink. The immersion of downward-moving fire in upward-moving water will result in the formation of a vapor. This is what is meant by the purification of ching in the transmutation of ch'i. When vapor (purified vital energy) rises and the heart is emptied of attachments and desire, the purified ch'i will rise to open the gate guarding the upper tan-t'ien. When this gate is unlocked, the purified shen, or spiritual energy, will emerge.

3. *The gathering of the herbs.* After the herbs (or flowers) emerge they need to be gathered and stored. If left alone, they will dissipate. Ching and ch'i may be stored in the bones and the lower and middle tan-t'iens. The energies may also be circulated through the meridians in the body. During this stage it is crucial not to let thoughts arise or else the herbs cannot be gathered. During the gathering of the herbs, the vapor must make one initial circulation through the meridians to complete a circuit. This process "collects" the three energies and merges them into the undifferentiated state of Earlier Heaven existence. With the union of the three energies the golden pill or elixir is formed.

4. *Sealing and containment.* After the herbs are gathered, the "container" must be sealed. This means that the openings where the treasures can dissipate must be closed. Our senses are the body's interface with the world. They are openings through which the internal universe communicates with the external environment. They are also the organs through which desire can be projected onto objects. Emotions such as anger will dissipate ch'i while the presence of desire will

dissipate the shen. "Sealing and containment" thus refers to dissolving emotions and desire.

5. *The Microcosmic Circulation.* This is the circulation of ching, ch'i, and shen through the tu and jen meridians.

6. *Cleansing.* The constant circulation of the energies through the tu and jen meridians will cleanse the body. The body is emptied of odors and the skin is coated with a shiny, oily surface. The cleansing also refers to clearing the heart of desire.

The alchemical changes described in *Cultivating Stillness* and its commentary are both physical and psychological phenomena. To underplay either of them is to lose the essence of the dual cultivation of body and mind that is central to Taoist thinking. My own understanding of many passages in this text was a result of the experience of changes within my body. In this I am indebted to my si-fu, who generously and patiently taught me the methods of the return to the Origin.

I

WU-CHI

太上老君著經

混然子　水精子　付圖註解

無極品第一

The ancient sage says, "The Tao has no form. It gives life to heaven and earth. The Tao is void of emotions. It moves the sun and moon. The Tao is nameless. It nourishes all things."

Commentary

The sage symbolizes the goodness inherent in all sentient beings. The origin of the ancient sage is difficult to fathom. He is the manifestation of the Tao and can appear in many forms. As the Elder Emperor of the Three Realms, he is called the Heavenly Teacher of the Ten Thousand Dharmas. As the Middle Emperor of the Three Realms he is called Pan-ku. As the Later Emperor of the Three Realms, he is called Chu-hua. During the time of the herbalist Shen-neng, he is the sage T'ai-hsing. In the era of the Yellow Emperor, he is the sage Kang-hsing. Since he takes on many forms it is difficult to enumerate all his incarnations. Sometimes he appears as a Confucian sage. Sometimes he appears as a buddha. Sometimes he appears as a Taoist immortal. His deeds are limitless. He is elusive and mysterious. He guides our intuition, instructs us in the virtues, and induces stillness in our hearts.

The Tao is supreme goodness. It has no form and is limitless. It is formless because there is no visible trace of its existence. The Tao is that energy that has existed from the beginning when there was neither structure nor differentiation. It is the source of life in heaven and on earth. It creates and nourishes all things. Yang vapor (energy) is symbolized by heaven and yin vapor by earth.

How does the Tao give life to heaven and earth? *Tzu* and *hai* are states of nondifferentiation and stillness. They are also called wu-chi. Tzu follows hai. In the emergence of tzu, movement stirs the stillness and yang is born. Yang vapor rises. In the universe it becomes heaven. In the human body it is the Mysterious Gate. *Ch'ou* follows tzu. In the transition to ch'ou, stillness emerges from movement and yin is born. Yin vapor sinks. In nature it becomes the earth. In the human body it is the tan-t'ien. Thus it is said that heaven emerges with tzu and earth rises with ch'ou.

The Tao is not affected by emotions. It belongs to the realm of Earlier Heaven and is without sound and smell. Emotions belong to the realm of Later Heaven. They are associated with planning and activity. In the path of inaction there are no emotions. The Tao guides the movement of the sun and moon. Movement follows a circulatory path. The sun is the Golden Raven. The moon is the Jade Rabbit. The sun belongs to the pa-k'ua position li and it symbolizes the cycle of the seasons. The moon belongs to the pa-k'ua position k'an and it symbolizes the cycle of waxing and waning. In the human body, li and k'an are the sacred sun and moon (the inner light of the two eyes) shining on the Golden Palace (the heart).

The Tao is nameless and has no form. It has no beginning and no end. When forced to give it a name, we call it the Tao. The Tao nurtures all things. Even insects and plants receive nourishment from the Tao. If human beings are willing to return to the Tao, they must find someone who can show them the heaven and earth, the sun and moon in their bodies. They must cultivate and follow the Tao that cannot be named. They must preserve and purify the precious ching (generative energy), ch'i (vital energy), and shen (spirit energy). Then they will be able to ascend to the High Pure, the Most Pure, and the Jade Pure Realms. They will reap the fruits of immortality, becoming heavenly immortals, golden immortals, or spirit immortals. They will live in peace, without being bound to earthly existence. They will live forever and not be subjected to reincarnation.

The sages say:

The Ancient Sage displays his esoteric wisdom in mysterious ways,
He gives us the true teachings in this scripture,
Ask your teacher to show you how to transcend life and death,
When you have received the instructions practice diligently to cultivate the dragon and tiger.
May everyone ascend to the pure still way,
May everyone rise to the lotus of many-colored auras.
After you are granted immortality in the palace of wu-ch'i,
You will become an immortal living in happiness.

This scripture is the boat that helps you cross the sea of earthly existence,

Beware! You can circle the five lakes and four seas aimlessly.
If the principles of the text are not revealed to you,
You will waste much time and effort and not harvest any fruit.
Miss one small part of the mystery,
And several decades will pass.
The sage has now revealed his teachings,
It is up to you to follow his instructions and arrive at the nine heavens.

Translator's Notes

1. The Elder, Middle, and Later Emperors are the Wu-ch'i T'ien-jun (the Lord of Wu-chi), the Ling-pao T'ien-jun (the Lord of the Precious Spirit), and the Tao-teh T'ien-jun (the Lord of Virtue). The domain of the Wu-chi T'ien-jun is wu-ch'i, a state of nondifferentiation, when things have not separated from the Tao. The domain of the Ling-pao T'ien-jun is t'ai-chi, where yin and yang have merged but are still rooted in the underlying unity of wu-chi. The domain of the Tao-teh T'ien-jun is the world in which differentiation has created the ten thousand myriad things. In the domain of the Wu-chi T'ien-jun, the Way of Heaven dominates. In the domain of the Ling-pao T'ien-jun, the Way of the Earth dominates. In the domain of the Tao-te T'ien-jun, the Laws of Humanity dominate. According to Taoist thinking, we are currently living in the domain of the Tao-te T'ien-jun.

2. The Three Pure Realms are: the Jade Pure *(yu-ch'ing)*, the Most Pure *(t'ai-ch'ing)*, and the High Pure *(shang-ch'ing)*. The Jade Pure Realm is the domain of the Wu-chi T'ien-jun. The Most Pure Realm is the domain of the Ling-pao T'ien-jun. The High Pure Realm is the domain of the Tao-te T'ien-jun.

The Jade Pure, the Most Pure, and the High Pure Realms represent three levels of enlightenment. To rise to the Jade Pure Realm is to attain wu-chi, the highest form of enlightenment. This is complete union with the Tao. To enter the Realm of the Great Pure is to exist in a state in which subject and object are differentiated but are integral parts of the Tao. It is a lesser form of enlightenment. To attain the Realm of the High Pure is to exist in harmony with nature and humanity, to live according to the laws of nature, and to embody the highest virtues of humanity. This is the lowest form of enlightenment.

3. Tzu, ch'ou, and hai are partitions within the Twelve Terrestrial Branches *(tzu, ch'ou, yin, mou, ch'en, ssu, wu, wei, hsin, yu, hsu, hai)*. The Twelve Terrestrial Branches mark the cycle of the years, months, and hours in the Chinese calendar. In alchemical Taoism, the Twelve Terrestrial Branches also describe the passage and cycles of internal energy in the body. Tzu is the first partition and hai is the last. Therefore, tzu and hai mark the transition of one cycle into the next. The transition of tzu to ch'ou, the next partition in the cycle, is the stirring of internal energy in the body. Internal energy continues to rise through yin, mou, ch'en, and ssu. At wu, it begins to fall and continues to reach its nadir at the transition from hsu to hai. From hai it is ready to start its next cycle again. The Twelve Branches not only describe the rise and fall of internal energy in the body. They also specify the pattern of energy movement through the seasons, the months, and the hours in the body and in nature.

2

WANG-CHI

皇極圖

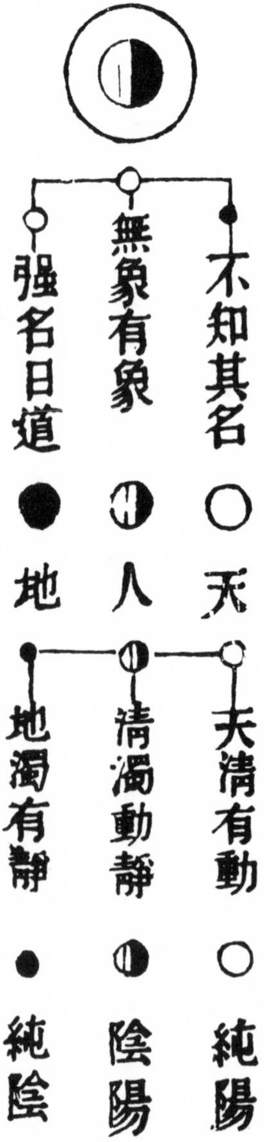

不知其名
無象有象
強名曰道

○ 天
◑ 人
● 地

天清有動
清濁動靜
地濁有靜

○ 純陽
◑ 陰陽
● 純陰

皇極品第二

I do not know its name. I am forced to call it Tao. The Tao has pure and impure aspects. Sometimes it is still. Sometimes it is moving. Heaven is pure and earth is impure. Heaven moves and earth is still.

Commentary

Lao-tzu says that the Tao has no form and no name. That is why he is forced to give it a name so that it can be referred to. Although the naming is said to be forced, force is used as a metaphor, for lack of a better descriptor. In fact, there is nothing forceful in this meaning, because he knows that the word *Tao* hides rich meanings. In the word *Tao* (道), we first write the two short slanting lines on top (⺌). The line on the left symbolizes the sun. The line on the right symbolizes the moon. It is like the t'ai-chi symbol, with yin and yang intertwined. In heaven, yang and yin are the sun and the moon. On earth, they are the Golden Raven and the Jade Rabbit. In the human body, they are the two eyes. In internal alchemy they are the outer and inner light reflecting on each other. The next stroke in the word *Tao* (道) is the horizontal line (一). This sign means "one." It symbolizes the circle wu-ch'i. In Earlier Heaven, this circle is ch'ien or pure yang. The *I Ching* says that "ch'ien is a circle." When the circle breaks, heaven is opened. The circle unfolds into a horizontal line. The *I Ching* says that "ch'ien is One." When heaven receives this Oneness it is pure. When earth receives this Oneness it is peaceful. When humans receive this Oneness they become sages. Confucianism says that "concentration is Oneness." Buddhism says that "all dharma comes from Oneness." Taoism says, "Hold onto the Origin and focus on Oneness." The next segment of the word *Tao* is (自). In this ideograph, *sun* (日) and *moon* (目) are contained in the word for "self" (自). The Confucian sages say, "In the word *Tao,* the top and bottom part of the character cannot be separated." If the parts are separated, it is no longer Tao. Combining the parts of the sign we have so far gives us the word (首), which means "foremost" or "most prior." This indicates that the cultivation of the Tao must be our foremost endeavor. Last of all we finish writing the word by adding in (辶). This ideograph symbolizes walking on a path. It represents the circulation of the dharmic wheel in our body. This is the meaning of the word *Tao*.

The Tao is the way of heaven. It is also our original nature. The energy of heaven is pure and the energy of earth is impure. Yang energy is always moving. Yin energy is static. The pure energy of heaven is yang. The impure energy of earth is yin. The moving heavens represent the circle of ch'ien. The static earth represents the stillness of k'un. Purity and impurity, motion and stillness, are manifested in the sun and moon in heaven, in spring and autumn on earth, and as sage and ordinary person in humankind. The sun is yang because it is always circular and full. The moon is yin because it waxes and wanes. Spring is yang because all things begin their growth in this season. Autumn is yin because all things begin to decay in this season. Sages are yang because when they shed their bodily shell they become immortal. Ordinary people are yin because when their lives end they become ghosts. These are the principles of purity and impurity, and motion and stillness.

If you do not know the meaning of pure and impure, if you do not know movement and stillness in your body, then you should quickly accumulate good deeds, petition the lords of heaven, and ask an enlightened teacher to show you the Tao in your body. You must let the light of the sacred sun and moon shine in it so that the impure energy sinks and the pure energy rises.

Sitting quietly and not moving is stillness. Craving is movement. If you are filled with desire and your senses are attached to objects, the heart is not still. Losing generative energy in sexual activity is movement. Storing generative energy is stillness. If you are free of cravings, in stillness you will see the mystery within.

The inner teachings must be transmitted orally and personally from teacher to student before they can be understood from the heart. If you practice the teachings diligently, immortality is not difficult to attain.

The sages say:

There is no text like *Cultivating Stillness,*
Store the generative energy and the principles will be clear.
Learn the contents of the chapters and you will transcend the three realms,
Honor the earth and protect the precious pearl.

The book *Cultivating Stillness*
Can guide even those who are evil and have gone astray,
And help them return to the path of the ways of heaven.
Immortality can be gained through the efforts of mortals.

Yin and yang, movement and stillness, are in heaven and in the human body,
In the empty center of wu-chi transform the lead into gold.
Know the methods of the rising and falling of the pure and impure,
And the bright light will chase away the night in the three thousand worlds.

Translator's Notes

1. *Wang-chi* is the intermediate state between wu-chi and t'ai-chi. Wu-chi is the undifferentiated state of the Void, or Tao, symbolized by the circle. T'ai-chi is the state of differentiation of the Tao into yin and yang where in yang there is yin and in yin there is yang. It is symbolized by the yin-yang swirls inside the circle with the white dot in the black swirl and the black dot in the white swirl. Wang-chi is the state of differentiation of the Tao into yin and yang in which yin and yang do not embody the essence of their opposites. Thus, the symbol of wang-chi is simply the two black and white swirls without the dots.

2. The Golden Raven and the Jade Rabbit symbolize the essence of yang and yin. The Golden Raven is the vapor of heaven. The Jade Rabbit is the vapor of earth. When the Raven descends and the Rabbit leaps up, a channel is open and the vapors of heaven and earth can form a circulatory flow. In internal alchemy this refers to the opening of the Microcosmic Orbit. They are also referred to as the Golden Boy and Jade Maiden.

3

T'AI-CHI

太極圖

陽儀　陰儀

坎西　離東

五行　順生

火
金　土　木
水

男動男清　女靜女濁

內

降本　流末

本
外
末

太極品第二

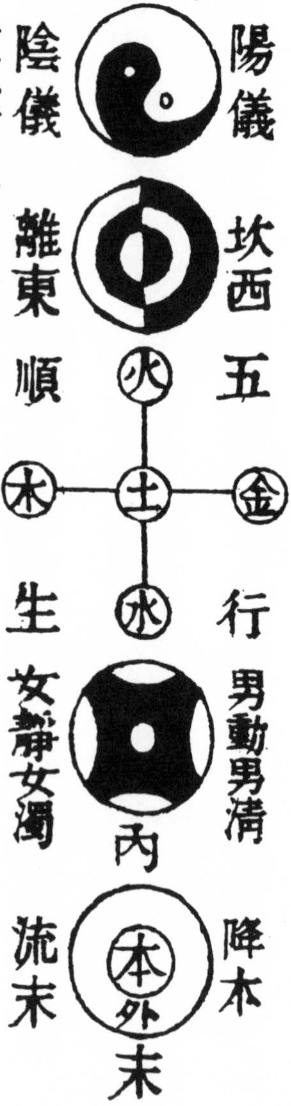

Male is pure and female is impure. Male is movement and female is stillness. In birth, growth, completion, and death, all things run their course.

Commentary

The discussion of male and female does not literally refer to men and women but to the ideas yin and yang. The male takes its form from ch'ien and the female takes its form from k'un. Ch'ien is pure and k'un is impure. Male is associated with the ancient yang. However, in yang there is yin. In the trigram *li*, there is incompleteness, as symbolized by the presence of the broken line in the middle of the solid lines in the trigram (☲). Female is associated with the ancient yin. However, in yin there is yang. In the trigram k'an, there is also incompleteness, as symbolized by the solid line in the midst of dotted lines in the trigram (☵). The male is purely yang at sixteen years of age and the essence of yin descends on the female at age fourteen. Pure yang is symbolized by the water element associated with jen. The essence of yin is in the water element associated with *kuei*. Jen is the white tiger and kuei is the green dragon. Thus in the teachings of the immortals there are methods of subduing the dragon and conquering the tiger. These are the ways of returning to the Tao and gaining immortality.

Male is associated with movement and female is associated with stillness. Male is the wind of heaven. Female is the vapor of earth. Therefore it is said that heaven moves and earth is still.

Humankind is the culmination of heaven and earth. Heaven and earth together are the source of humankind. Thus, humankind must not forget its beginning and its end. The source of heaven and earth is the Tao. It gives birth to all things. When heaven and earth do not lose their connection with the source, they exist forever. When humans do not lose their connection to the source, they become immortals and their life span is like that of heaven and earth.

From times of old it has been said that people must die. However, in the *Spring and Autumn Annals* it is said that "if humans can open the Mysterious Gate, then they will not die." Immortality is in the spirit (shen). The scriptures say, "All things have a source and an end; all events have a beginning and an end. Know this sequence and you will be near the Tao. The gate that gives me life is the gate that gives me death. Only a few understand this intuitively. At night the Iron Guardian dominates your thoughts. Immortality can be achieved with human effort." The Mysterious Gate has many names. In Confucianism, it is called the altar of wisdom. It embodies limitless compassion. It is a consciousness without thoughts and it reflects the way of heaven. It is intuitive knowledge and reflects the way of earth. In Buddhism, the Mysterious Gate is the spirit mountain, the empty consciousness of original mind, or nirvana, the realm of the Amitabha Buddha. In Taoism, it is the Golden Palace, the realm of t'ai-chi, the domain of the Three Pure Realms, the root of existence of all things. Although it is given different names by the three religions, it is nonetheless the same thing. In Confucianism, when this gate is opened, the sage emerges. In Buddhism, when this gate is opened, the Buddha emerges. In Taoism, when this gate is opened, the immortal emerges. Opening the Mysterious Gate is a guarded secret. That is why the teachers of the three religions did not reveal it casually. They feared that ignorant and unethical persons would use this knowledge to defile the Tao, thus angering the guardians of the Tao and bringing destruction to the world. If you are sincere in seeking this knowledge, you must look for a teacher and humbly ask your teacher to show you the opening of the Mysterious Gate. From then on, if your actions follow the Tao, you will progress. If your actions stray from the Tao, your progress will be halted. If you think that the Mysterious Gate is only the physical location at the *ni-wan* on your brow, or the solar plexus, or the tan-t'ien in your abdomen, or the cavity positioned between your kidneys, or at the base of your spine, then you are mistaken, for the Tao is not located in these places.

The sages say:

Female and male, impure and pure,
Return to the origin and search for the true feeling,
Action is associated with the sun and movement, and inaction is associated with stillness,
Receive the source and your years will be lengthened; lose the source and you will lose everything.

Hurry, turn back to the origin and cultivate compassion,
Take advantage of the fact that the breath of life is still present and learn the art of immortality.
Although you may accumulate gold and property,
You leave the world with empty hands.

T'ai-chi, yin and yang, are very mysterious.
Very few people know of the path of immortality.
If mortals in this world do not want to die,
They must lengthen their lives, add oil to the lamp, and preserve the great harmony.

Translator's Note

The *Spring and Autumn Annals* is a book recording the historical events and ceremonial practices in the Kingdom of Lu during the Spring and Autumn period (770–476 B.C.E.) of the Eastern Chou dynasty (770–221 B.C.E.). It is one of the Confucianist classics.

4

The THREE REALMS *of* EXISTENCE

三才圖

陽中有陰　陰中有陽　靜中有動

天

動中有靜　陽中有陰　陰中有陽

清者濁之源

動者靜之基

三才品第四

The origin of purity lies in impurity. Movement is the foundation of stillness.

Commentary

That which is pure is weightless. That which is impure is heavy. Stillness is inaction and movement is action. Heaven consists of rising vapors. These vapors originate from earth and ascend upwards. Earth is yin and impure in nature. Moving to its extreme, yin gives way to yang. When impurities settle in stillness purity emerges.

The yang body is pure and the yin body is impure. The pure body originates from the impure body. In Taoist alchemy, spirit is pure yang. However, the origin of the spirit is in the impurity of mundane generative energy transmuted into purified generative energy. Purified generative energy, which is yang in nature, is then transmuted into vital energy, and from vital energy the spirit emerges. We cultivate generative energy to transform it into vital energy; we cultivate vital energy to transform it into spirit energy. This is purity originating in impurity.

If you wish to return to the Tao you must rid the body of impurities. Let the pure air rise to form the golden pill and let the impurities sink. Accumulate good deeds and study the scriptures so that you will transcend the world and be free of earthly existence.

Many people are ignorant and do not recognize their original nature. They say that it is impossible for mortals to become immortal. However, in reality, the Tao is not far from human existence and human existence is never far from the Tao. People destroy themselves and willingly live in suffering. They do not realize that we owe our origin to yin and yang and the five elements. Of all beings, humans possess the spark of intelligence. We are capable of embodying heaven and earth. Heaven and earth are manifested in the sun and moon, and the motion of the sun and moon is manifested in yin and yang, in waning and waxing. When yang wanes, yin waxes. In the ordinary person, when yang dissipates totally and yin dominates, the human becomes a ghost. In the sage, yang rises and yin diminishes. When yin dissipates totally and pure yang dominates, the human becomes an immortal. Mortal beings are therefore half yin and half yang, half immortal and half ghost. If you cultivate yourself and rid yourself of impurities then you will be become an immortal.

Mencius says that the ancient sages are no different from anyone else. This means that everyone can become a sage, a buddha, or an immortal. It depends on whether you have the will and discipline. If you have the motivation, then you can cultivate immortality in the home or in the monastery. If you are training at home, then your spouse is your friend and your children are your companions. Although your existence is in the mortal realm, your heart transcends it. If you understand these teachings, then immortality is not difficult to attain.

The sages say:

See through the illusions of life and understand their emptiness,
The sun hides inside the bright moon.
If humans understand the principles of yin and yang,
Then they can master the foundations of heaven.
Empty your mind and fill your belly to seek the golden lead,
Inside the moon you can clearly see the sun.
Open the pathway in which yang rises and yin descends,
The golden pill will emerge and fragrance will cover your body.

The purity of the male and the impurity of the female have their counterparts in Earlier Heaven.
Many do not know the origins and stray from the natural way.
The woman must slay the dragon and the man must conquer the tiger.
Why do you worry that mortals cannot achieve immortality?

5

The MIND (HEART) *of* TAO

道心圖

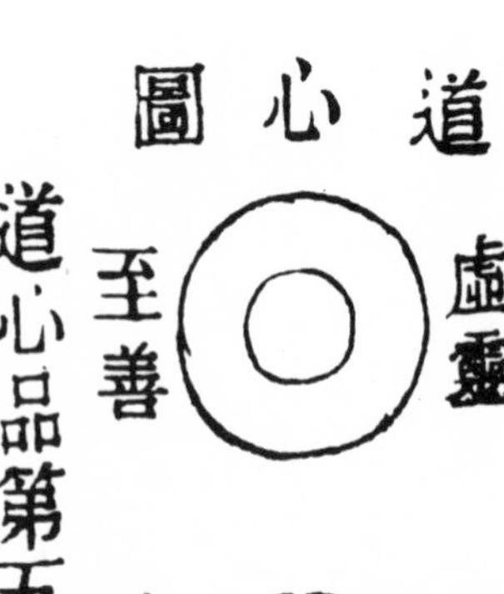

上藥三品
神與氣精

道心品第五

If people can constantly be pure and still, then heaven and earth will return to their places.

Commentary

Those who cultivate the Tao regard purity and stillness as supreme. Do not see that which is not virtuous and your eyes will be pure and still. Do not hear that which is not virtuous and your ears will be pure and still. Do not say that which is not virtuous and your mouth will be pure and still. Do not do that which is not virtuous and your heart will be pure and still.

What is meant by "heaven and earth will return to their places"? If you have instructions from an enlightened teacher, then in the microcosm of your body, the vapor of heaven will return to earth. Mercury of the earth will become lead. The vapor of earth will return to heaven. The lead of heaven will become mercury. Generative energy resides in the North Sea. Practice the art of purity and stillness and the let heavenly breath in the body return to its place. Then the breath of heaven outside the body will follow this course. Spirit lives in the Southern Mountain. Practice the art of purity and stillness and let the earthly breath return to its place. Then the breath of the earth outside the body will follow this course as well.

The heaven of the body is the mind (or heart) of Tao. In Earlier Heaven, the mind of Tao is ch'ien and ch'ien is heaven. This is why the mind of Tao is called heaven. In Earlier Heaven, the North Sea is k'un and k'un is earth. This is why the North Sea is called earth. Ch'ien and k'un are the heaven and earth of our body. When heaven and earth, when the inside and outside of the body resonate with each other and are guided by the same master, the breath of heaven and the breath of earth will return to the origin. If there is no guide, then the breath of heaven and earth in our body will flow out of us. Not only can we not achieve union with the Tao, but the Tao will be damaged.

The scriptures say: "The mind of Tao is inconspicuous and the ways of the human mind are devious. The instructions that guard the Mysterious Gate teach people to distance themselves from the devious mind. The mind that tries to cultivate the Tao but remains attached to the world; the person who does not receive instructions from an enlightened teacher but only looks for the Tao in books, does not recognize the Tao as supreme and precious." Tzu-kung, a student of Confucius, says: "The written word can be heard and obtained, but teachings of the Tao cannot be obtained in the written word." The honorable person is concerned with the Tao and not with riches. The Tao that is coded in words is dead. The teachings of the Tao are so precious and important that they cannot be revealed in the written word. That the

Tao can be revealed indiscriminantly to honorable and dishonorable persons alike is unthinkable and unreasonable. The scriptures of the sages of the three religions (Confucianism, Buddhism, and Taoism) teach us how to rule the country, manage the family, and interact with other people. The book *Cultivating Stillness* explains that in cultivating the body and mind, it is important to hide and not to reveal. That which is revealed is but the mundane mind that does not have wisdom. Those who do not know state that the Yellow Palace is three and six-tenths inches below the heart, that the cavity between the kidneys is the body of the Earlier Heaven, or that the emptied heart is the mind of Tao. They only talk about the return to the Tao. It is a pity that mortals believe all these words to be the truth.

The sages say:

It is a pity that sentient beings misrecognize the mind,
They think the Yellow Palace is a position in the body,
They stray from the Way and never see spring and summer,
In the nine regions of the earth there are few believers.
You must end your wrongs in the path of the immortals,
And from the path purge all coldness and yin,
Step carefully between the shores of good and evil,
The compassionate ones rise and the cruel ones fall.

The mind of Tao is inconspicuous and the human mind is devious.
Few are pure and few have the wisdom.
In the center of compassion is the place of union,
Inside the Mysterious Gate is the realm of *yao-chi*.
Lock up the monkey and ape so they cannot run away.
Tame the wild horse so that it cannot get out of control.
Grasp the opening of the Gate and when cultivation is complete,

The beam of golden light will penetrate your entire being.

Translator's Notes

1. The Golden Palace is the middle tan-t'ien where the transmutation of ching to ch'i takes place. The middle tan-t'ien also acts as a storage place for purified vital energy.

2. The North Sea is the Sea of Ch'i, an area along the jen meridian where purified generative energy is stored. Taoist internal alchemy views the human body as an eight-point compass. The lower part of the body is north and the upper part is south. The Sea of Ch'i is the storage area for generative energy. Some Taoist texts say that the internal alchemical changes occur in the lower tan-t'ien but the refined product is stored in the area around the Sea of Ch'i. Energy can be brought out of storage. The stirring of the Sea of Ch'i is the movement of the energy from storage to other parts of the body.

Other Taoist texts say that the lower tan-t'ien is a field consisting of an area which includes the point called the tan-t'ien, the Winding River, and the Sea of Ch'i. The movement of energy that occurs in the lower tan-t'ien while it is being purified is often described as tossing the tan-t'ien. The process is likened to whipping up waves in the Winding River and the Sea of Ch'i.

3. The Southern Mountain is an area along the jen meridian centered on the middle tan-t'ien. When the fires of the Southern Mountain sink and the waters of the North Sea rise, the resulting alchemical process is called the immersion of fire in water or the exchange of li and k'an. In internal alchemy, this is the transmutation of purified generative energy into vital energy using breath as a catalyst.

4. Yao-chi is the domain of the Wu-chi T'ien-jun. It is used interchangeably with wu-chi.

6

The HUMAN MIND (HEART)

識神

不生不滅

至虛至靈

頭心

人心品第六

The spirit tends toward purity, but the mind disturbs it.

Commentary

What is it meant by "the spirit tends toward purity"? Humans consist of one half yang and one half yin. When the word *human* (人) receives the "One" (一), it becomes "Great" (大). When *Great* (大) receives the "One" (一) it becomes "Heaven" (天). Humans are created from the descent of heavenly breath and the ascent of earthly vapor. Humankind emerges from the union of yin and yang. The spirit is the original nature in us. When humans contact earthly air, knowledge emerges in them. Opposed to knowledge is the spirit. The spirit is formless and is incomprehensible to mundane thoughts. It governs the life-maintaining functions of the body. Knowledge is active, mischievous, and intelligent. It changes constantly. Spirit, on the other hand, is the master of humankind. Its origin is in wu-chi. In Taoism it is called the Iron Guardian. In Buddhism it is called the Golden Arhat. In Confucianism it is called the soul. It is never born and it never dies. When it leaves the body it becomes a ghost. Cultivate compassion and it will become an immortal or a buddha. Do evil deeds and it will become an animal.

The existence of the spirit is connected with the existence of the body. It emerges with conception in the mother's womb. It rises from wu-chi and controls the functioning of the body. When the ten months of pregnancy are over, the infant utters a cry and falls to the ground. Here the spirit descends from wu-chi into the flesh and blood of the infant. Simultaneously, with the first breath, knowledge enters the infant's body to dwell with the spirit in the mind. From then on, knowledge takes control of the human being and the spirit loses its place. The seven emotions and the six desires arise. Day and night the spirit dissipates until it disappears. Earth, water, fire, and wind gradually lose their strength and the body loses vitality. Knowledge is part of the self. When the body dies it leaves the shell. Even if you live to over one hundred, life is still a dream. At death the ghosts will escort the spirit to hell. There, good and evil deeds accumulated during your lifetime are evaluated and you will be rewarded or punished accordingly. The good will be given another lifetime on earth to enjoy earthly happiness, or will become ghosts and receive offerings or incense. The evil will be given another lifetime to reap the punishment allotted to them, or be reincarnated as animals and not escape the ten thousand *kalpas* (lifetimes).

The spirit tends toward purity and stillness. Knowledge

tends toward action and disturbs the mind so that it cannot be still. As this continues, the body and mind are injured. When the spirit weakens, a hundred illnesses arise. Therefore, we need to realize the value of the human body. We need to appreciate the fortune of being born in the human form and the fortune of encountering the teachings of the Buddha and the Tao. You who are born in human form should not spend your time foolishly. You must value your original nature and your life. Recognize the difference between spirit and knowledge. Do not confuse the true with the false. Recognize the difference between the human mind and the mind of Tao. Do not mistake the human mind for the mind of Tao, and knowledge for the spirit. Do not mistake the false body for the true body.

In the Buddhist scriptures it is said that the word *mind* (心) has three dots (丶丶丶) resembling the shape of stars. It has a sickle-shaped ideograph (乚) that resembles the crescent moon. It is from here that everything begins. Even the Buddha emerges from the mind. Immortal Lü says: "Existence in human form is difficult to achieve and you already have it. The Tao is difficult to find. If you do not transcend human existence now, when you will you get a better chance?"

The sages say:

The mind of Tao is contained in the books of Confucius,
In purity and stillness your spirit will be revealed.
The true scriptures and dharmas all teach the Tao,
The principles of heaven and the cycles of the years are in the philosophy of Confucianism.
The emperor Wu of Han sought to live a thousand years,
The emperor of Ch'in fantasized about a kingdom lasting ten thousand years.

If you study this text you can bid farewell to spring and
autumn,
For ch'ien and k'un will safely guard the jade vessel.

The various scriptures reveal extraordinary thoughts,
Open them systematically and you will see the wonders.
Now that spring and autumn have passed,
You only wait for morning and evening to fill the emptiness.
Rely on purity and stillness as the remedy,
How can the purple mushroom grow from the human
mind?
The mind of Tao is your true father and mother,
And the centering energy is your precious child.

7

The Six Thieves

六賊品第七

The mind tends toward stillness but it is opposed by craving.

Commentary

The human mind does not have an innate tendency toward stillness. However, because the spirit dwells in it, the mind is still when the spirit is in control. The human mind does not have an innate tendency toward activity. But, because knowledge dwells in it, the mind is active when knowledge is in control. Because there are six residues in the human body, there arise six impulses. The six impulses produce the six dusts. Because there are the six dusts, the six thieves emerge. Because of the existence of the six thieves, the six spirits wither. Because the six spirits wither, the human form falls into the six existences.

The six thieves are these: the eyes, ears, nose, tongue, body, and mind. If the eyes crave beauty and enticement, then the soul will fall into the hell of those born from eggs and will be reincarnated as a bird. Its colorful plumage will be watched by all. Is that not good to see? If the ears want to hear evil things, the soul will fall into the hell of those born of the womb. You will be reincarnated as a mule, horse, camel, or other beast of burden who wears bells on its harness. Is that not good to hear? If the nose craves fragrant smells, the soul will fall into the hell of those born in wet realms. You will be reincarnated as a crab, shrimp, prawn, or other creature that lives in the muck at the bottom of the sea. It will always live in dirty and foul-smelling environments. Is that not good to smell? If the tongue craves the five tastes, the soul will fall into the hell of those born as insects. You will be reincarnated as a mosquito, fly, or wasp. The mouth will be the instrument causing harm to others. Is that not good to taste? If the heart craves riches, the soul will fall into the hell of those born with hooves. You will be reincarnated as a bearer of goods such as a camel. All your life you will have treasures strapped to your back. Is that not wealth? If your body craves sexual activity, the soul will descend to the hell of those born who mate continuously. You will be reincarnated as a chicken, duck, or turkey and will always have sexual interactions. Is that not enjoyable? These are the consequences of the six cravings.

You also need to know of the seven emotions and the seven injuries. The seven emotions are these: happiness, anger, sadness, fear, love, cruelty, desire. Excessive happiness injures the heart. Excessive anger injures the liver. Excessive sadness injures the lungs. Excessive fear injures the gall bladder. Excessive love injures the spirit. Excessive cruelty injures sensitivity. Excessive desires injure the spleen. These are the relations between the seven emotions and the seven injuries.

There are also the ten weaknesses. Walk too much and the tendons will weaken. Stand too much and the bones will weaken. Sit too much and the blood will weaken. Sleep too much and the meridians will weaken. Listen too much and the generative force will weaken. See too much and the spirit will weaken. Speak too much and vital energy will weaken. Eat too much and the heart will weaken. Think too much and the spleen will weaken. Too much sex will dissipate generative energy. These are the ten weaknesses.

All mortals are affected by the destructive effects of the six thieves, the seven emotions, and the ten weaknesses. Eradicate the six thieves, the seven emotions, the ten losses and you will return to the Tao mind. Do not let the six thieves drag you into the dark realms of suffering.

The sages say:

See no visual enticements and smell no fragrance,
Concentrate and cultivate original nature sincerely.
When the three realms are empty without a trace of any existence,
When nothing is born and nothing dies, your life will lengthen.

If you do not stop craving the spirit will depart,
When the spirit departs the six thieves will disturb the heart and tan-t'ien.
When the heart and tan-t'ien are disturbed then the body has no guide,
Reincarnation in the six existences will always be in front of you.

The light of the spirit shines through the night of samsara,
The commoner and the sage both come from the same family.
Stop all cravings and the pristine body will appear,
The movement of the six thieves is like clouds that cover the sky.

8

The Three Obstructions

三尸圖

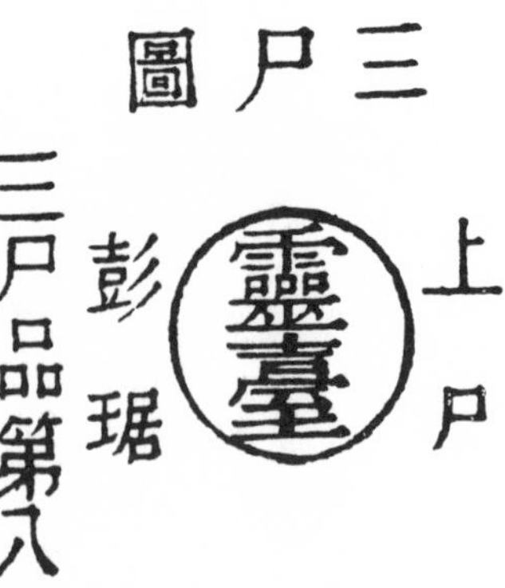

三尸品第八

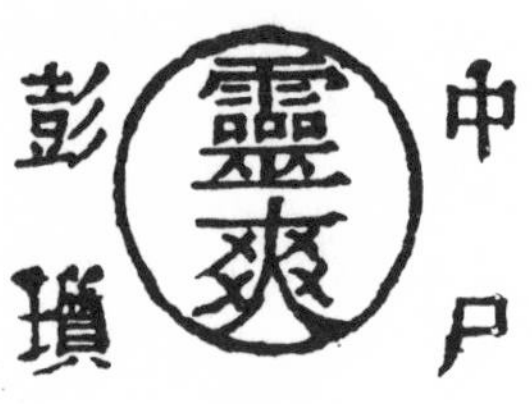

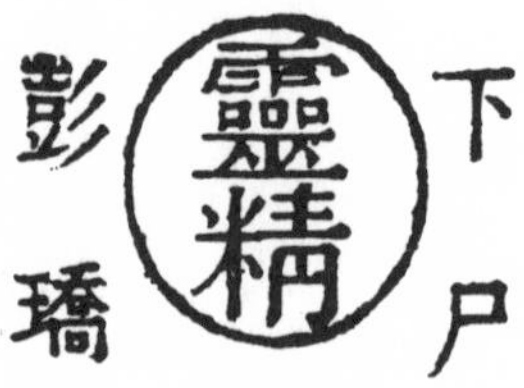

If you are able to control desire, then the mind will be still. Clear the mind and the spirit will be pure. Accordingly, the six cravings will not emerge and the three poisons will disappear.

Commentary

Desires are egotistic cravings. In the second and sixth hour, clean and clear the altar of the spirit. Do not let the ten thousand myriad things disturb it. In this way the forms outside will not enter and the treasures inside will not exit. Then the mind will be pure and still.

Clearing the mind is like removing residue from water. When the mind has desire, it is like water mixed with dirt and mud. Know how to stop craving and your foundation will be stable. When the foundation is stable, then the mind can be still. The Fifth Patriarch of Buddhism says: "The body is the bodhi tree. The heart is the stand of the clear mirror. It must be swept constantly so that dust cannot settle on it." The Sixth Patriarch says: "The bodhi is originally not a tree and the clear mirror has no stand. Since there is nothing to begin with, how can dust settle?"

What is meant by "purifying the spirit"? When there is not a thought in the mind, the spirit is pure. When the spirit is pure, no craving arises in the eyes, ears, nose, tongue, heart, and body. The three poisons are the three obstacles. In the human body there are three monsters. They are also known as the three poisons. The upper monster monitors good and evil in the Upper Burning Space. The middle monster monitors good and evil in the Middle Burning Space. The lower monster monitors good and evil in the Lower Burning Space. The upper monster resides in the upper gate (where the spine enters the skull). The middle monster resides in the middle gate (in the spine between the shoulder blades). The lower monster resides in the lower gate (in the spine between the kidneys). During the times of *keng, shen, chia,* and *tzu* the monsters report our deeds to the Jade Emperor.

There are also nine worms that cause much destruction. They block the three gates and the nine cavities so that the true yang cannot rise. The first worm is the prostrating worm and it lives in the *yu-chen* (also known as the *feng-fu* cavity). The second worm is the dragon worm and it lives in the cavity *t'ien-chu*. The third worm is the white worm and it lives in the cavity *tao-tao*. The fourth worm is the flesh worm and it lives in the cavity *shen-tao*. The fifth worm is the green worm and it lives in the cavity *chi-chung*. The sixth worm is the worm of hindrance and it lives in the cavity *hsuan-shu*. The seventh worm is the lung worm and it resides in the *ming-men*. The eighth worm is the stomach worm and it resides in the *yang-kuan* cavity. The ninth worm is the golden-scale bug and it lives in the cavity *wei-lu*.

The three monsters reside in the three gates and the nine worms live in the nine cavities. They manifest themselves in all manner of shapes. They can appear as beautiful objects in waking life, as spirits in dreams, and as fantasy worlds. They cause worries during sleeping and waking and make it difficult for people to return to the Tao. That is why the scriptures say: "The three monsters and the nine worms live in the body. They hinder the flow of the Yellow River and let the poisons penetrate deeply. Open the three gates, destroy the nine worms, and you will gain long life." If you want to cultivate the Tao you must slay the three monsters and kill the nine worms. You must hurry and seek an enlightened teacher to show you the Tao. Ask the Monkey Lord to get the golden staff from the Dragon Palace of the Eastern Sea to break open the three gates. Ask the Pig Immortal to use his rake to wrench open the nine cavities. When the three monsters lose their shapes and the nine worms disappear, then the gates and cavities will be open and the dharmic wheel can circulate without stopping. The roots of your original nature will exist forever and the foundation of your life will be stable. The seven emotions will be inactive; the six cravings will not emerge; and the three poisons will decrease and dissipate forever.

The sages say:

Meditating in a thatched monastery is better than living in a grand building,
Slay the three guards and ascend to the ten regions.
Shun jade, jewelry, and guests with golden horses,
And bury your fancy poetry and clothing in the mountain wilderness.

The seven emotions and six cravings are like dust borne by the wind,
In one night they will cover all that is new.

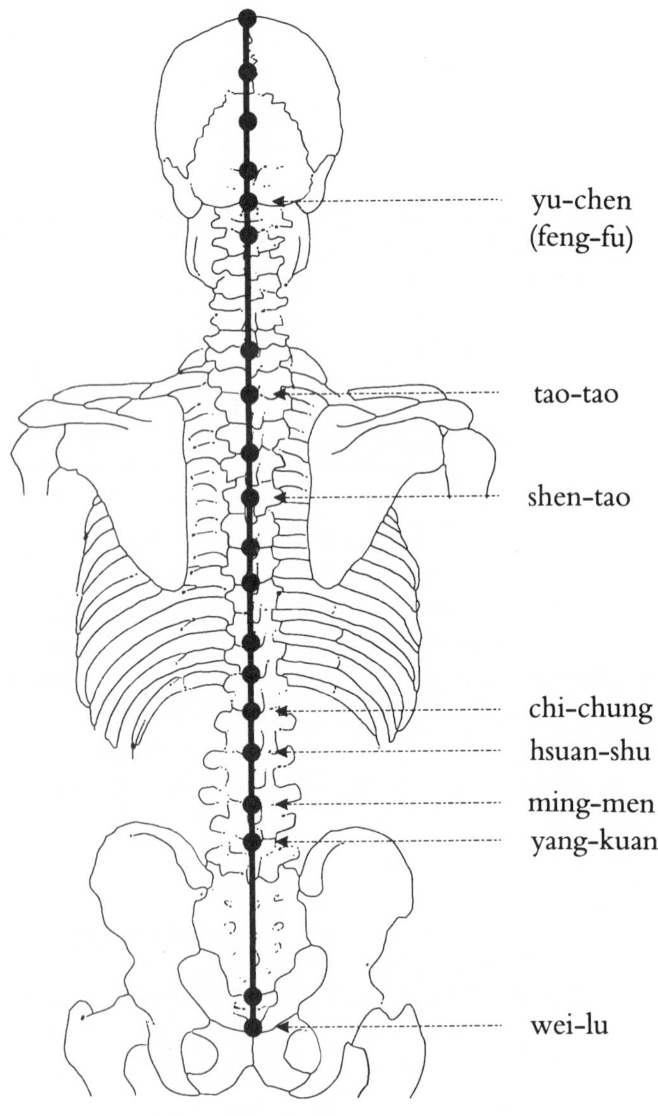

Figure 3.

The worm cavities and the gates along the tu meridian.

If you wait till the earth thunder begins to shake,
The shouts of the three guards and screams of ghosts will
be fearful to hear.

When the first yang rises use your effort,
Use this opportunity to eradicate the nine worms and
three monsters.
Take care when you are fighting them in battle,
Or you will sink to the bottom of Tung-ting Lake.

Translator's Notes

1. Keng and chia are two of the Ten Celestial Stems. The Celestial Stems mark the position of the constellations at the beginning of the new lunar year. For example, chia denotes the position of, say Taurus, in a certain location in the sky in the beginning of a new lunar year; keng will denote Taurus in a different location. When Taurus returns to its first location, the cycle of the Ten Celestial Stems begins again. The Ten Celestial Stems are *chia, i, ping, ting, wu, chi, keng, hsin, jen, kuei.* Five of Stems are yin—i, ting, chi, hsin, kuei; and five are yang—chia, ping, wu, keng, jen. Each stem is associated with a number and a position in the pa-k'ua. Chia is three and i is eight and they are associated with the east. Ting is two and ping is seven and they are associated with the south. Wu is five and chi is ten and they are associated with the center. Hsin is four and keng is nine and they are associated with the west. Jen is one and kuei is six and they are associated with the north. Stems with the odd numbers are yang and stems with the even numbers are yin. Thus, to each of the positions of the pa-k'ua mentioned above there is a pair of yin and yang. See also chapter 21 and table 3 (page 50) for further references on the Ten Celestial Stems.

2. Tzu and shen are two of the Twelve Terrestrial Branches.

The Twelve Terrestrial Branches denote the twelve months of the year and the twenty-four hours of the day divided into two-hour segments. Generally, the Twelve Terrestrial Branches have been used to mark the passage of time into fractions of twelve. The Twelve Terrestrial Branches are: *tzu, ch'ou, yin, mao, ch'en, ssu, wu, wei, shen, yu, hsu, hai*. The Ten Celestial Stems and Twelve Terrestrial Branches together form the sixty-year Sexagenary Cycle. Lining up the Ten Celestial Stems with the Twelve Terrestrial Branches until the first pair is repeated will result in sixty pairs. The sixty pairs are also used to mark a cycle of sixty days. The days *chia-tzu* and *keng-shen* (the first and fifty-seventh days of each sixty-day cycle) are times in which the monsters (or worms) report the deeds of each individual to the Jade Emperor.

3. The worms are responsible for illness. On the days chia-tzu and keng-shen the doors of heaven are opened. The worms report to the Jade Emperor what they have observed in the human realm during the past sixty-day cycle. The worms are eager to report evil deeds of an individual because wrongdoings diminish longevity. The sooner the individual dies, the sooner the worms are liberated from the body to become wandering spirits, stealing offerings from temples, graves, and shrines. To eradicate the worms, an individual needs to accumulate good deeds and regain health. As the internal organs strengthen and the Three Treasures are purified, the worms are destroyed. They can no longer plague the body with illness or create havoc in the spirit world.

9

The Nature *of* Emotion

氣質圖

氣質品第九

性

哀

怒

欲

喜

樂

心

Those who are unable to attain the Tao are those whose minds are not clear and who are still slaves of their emotions.

Commentary

Those who are unable to attain the Tao are people whose minds are not clear. Those who are slaves of their emotions are people who are not free of the seven emotions and six cravings. Mortals are unable to become immortals, buddhas, or sages because they cannot lay aside happiness, anger, sadness, delight. Be free of the emotion happiness and it will be transformed into original nature. Be free of the emotion anger and it will be transformed into original feeling. Be free of the emotion sadness and it will be transformed into original spirit.

Be free of the emotion delight and it will be transformed into original generative force. Be free of want and it will be transformed into the original breath. In this way the five cravings will be transformed into the five original essences. When this happens, you will become immortal.

The Confucian sages say: "See not that which you abstain from; hear not that which stirs up your fears." The Buddhists teach that there should be no thoughts in the eyes, ears, nose, tongue, and body; no color, no sound, no fragrance, no taste, and no touch. The Taoists say that forms are elusive. The three religions teach the same principles. Act according to the three teachings and you will be free of craving.

Craving is yin. The three religions all teach people to cultivate pure yang because immortals are said to be of pure yang. Follow the path of yin and you will become a ghost. Follow the path of yang and you will become an immortal. Taoist internal alchemy teaches us to accumulate yang fire in the morning and expel yin energy in the evening. If you do not know the methods of accumulating yang fire and expelling yin energy, then you must let go of the material world and accumulate good deeds to move the lords of heaven. You must find an enlightened teacher to show you your original nature and instruct you in the methods of accumulating yang fire and dispelling yin energy. Original nature and the Way of Heaven are not simply understood when heard. The teachings are given orally but must be received by the heart.

On the first day of every (lunar) month, the sun and moon are in conjunction. The first yang emerges in the hour of tzu on the third day. Its name is the Earth-thunder of the trigram fu. In the hai hour of the fifth day, the second yang emerges. Its name is the Earth-lake of the trigram lin. When the tzu hour of the eighth day arrives, the third yang emerges. Its name is Earth-heaven of the trigram t'ai. It is also eight measures of lead. At the hai hour of the tenth day, the fourth

TABLE I.

	Hour	Hexagram	
tzu	(11 P.M.–1 A.M.)	fu	䷗
ch'ou	(1 A.M.–3 A.M.)	lin	䷒
yin	(3 A.M.–5 A.M.)	t'ai	䷊
mao	(5 A.M.–7 A.M.)	chuang	䷡
ch'en	(7 A.M.–9 A.M.)	kuai	䷪
ssu	(9 A.M.–11 A.M.)	ch'ien	䷀
wu	(11 A.M.–1 P.M.)	k'ou	䷫
wei	(1 P.M.–3 P.M.)	tun	䷠
shen	(3 P.M.–5 P.M.)	pi	䷋
yu	(5 P.M.–7 P.M.)	kuan	䷓
hsu	(7 P.M.–9 P.M.)	po	䷖
hai	(9 P.M.–11 P.M.)	k'un	䷁

The twelve hexagrams and the hours of the day.

yang emerges. Its name is Thunder-heaven of the trigram chuang. At the tzu hour of the thirteenth day, the fifth yang emerges. Its name is the Lake-heaven of the trigram kuai. At the hai hour of the fifteenth day, the sixth yang emerges. Its name is ch'ien of the trigram of the same name. The *I Ching* says that the honorable person is ch'ien in nature. *Ch'ien* refers to a body of pure yang. If you do not cultivate your body and refine it with fire, then after this period yin will rise.

With the arrival of the hour of tzu on the eighteenth day, the first yin emerges. Its name is Heaven-wind of the trigram kou. At the hai hour of the twentieth day, the second yin emerges. Its name is Heaven-mountain of the trigram tun. At the tzu hour of the twenty-third day, the third yin emerges. Its name is Heaven-earth of the trigram pi. It is also eight measures of mercury. When the hai hour of the twenty-fifth day arrives, the fourth yin emerges. Its name is Wind-earth of the trigram kuan. At the hour of tzu on the twenty-eighth day, the fifth yin emerges. Its name is Mountain-earth of the trigram po. At the hai hour of the thirtieth day, the sixth yin emerges. Its name is k'un of the trigram of the same name. The six lines of the trigram are all yin, and all yang energies are buried in the earth. The sky has no moon. When there is no moon, there is no life.

The sages say:

My ways of cultivating the Tao involve accumulating yang,
In the Ho-to are important messages,
Even numbers symbolize greed and odd numbers symbolize the Tao,
Get rid of desire and yin will disappear and yang will grow.
If you receive the true teachings of the principles of wu-chi
The pill will grow naturally and your body will smell of fragrance,
One day you will emerge from the womb,
And leap outside mundane existence into the realm of the Jade Emperor.

The cultivation of the original nature requires training in the ways of heaven,

The moon waxes and wanes spanning the west and south.
Decrease the yin and the pill will ripen,
The yang fire will grow and the moon will become full.
Open k'an and fill li to return to the original existence.
Capture the bird and the rabbit to regain the original city.
From now on I shall not enter the Palace of the Lord of the Dead.
I shall become an immortal and travel to the Jade Palace.

10

Nothingness

虛無圖

內觀其心

心

心無其心

虛無品第十

外觀其形

形

形無其形

遠觀其物

物

物無其物

Look into your mind and there is no mind. Look at appearances and appearances have no forms. Gaze at distant objects and objects do not exist. Understand these three modes of cognition and you will see emptiness.

Commentary

Gaze within yourself. All thoughts arise from the mind. If there are no thoughts, then there is no mind. Thoughts emerge from forms. If there are no forms, then no thoughts can arise. Look at the sky, earth, sun, moon, stars, mountains, rivers, and buildings. When these objects do not exist then forms do not exist.

When mind, body, and things are extinguished, then there is only emptiness. Emptiness is the condition of existence in which heaven, earth, humankind, and all things are undifferentiated. What is meant by "seeing emptiness"? Outwardly, it refers to neutrality. Inwardly, it refers to the true void that is the Mysterious Gate in the body. The Taoist texts say: "Within the three realms, only the Tao is supreme." The Old Patriarch says: "Problems arise because I have a body. If I do not have my body, then what problems are there?" He also says: "Place little importance on your body so that it can be most important; abandon your body so that it can be preserved." The *Diamond Sutra* says: "You cannot see the Tathagata Buddha with your body." Zen Master Rinzai says: "Real things have no form; real nature has no substance; the real Dharma has no features." The immortals say: "Do not confuse your mundane body with the Tao. Beyond this body is the real body."

Since ancient times, those who have attained the Tao to become immortals and buddhas have practiced concentration and forgetting. In this world, many people are attached to appearances and think that their physical body is the original body. They use wine and meat to fatten their bodies. They cover their bodies with beautiful clothing. They want sexual gratification. Even if they cultivate their bodies, they only practice the Eight Devas (yoga), the Six Breathing Techniques, and the Lesser Microcosmic Circulation. They only know how to manipulate the mundane body. Or they eat herbs such as the Three Grasses, or ingest chemicals, thinking that they can cultivate the pill externally. Or they engage in sexual yoga, using the bodies of young women as the stove and cauldron. They absorb the sexual energy and generative force of the woman, thinking that they can use the yin energy to cultivate yang energy. Or they drink the generative fluid, thinking that it will strengthen their brains. Or they ingest chemicals such as cinnabar, thinking that it is the peach of Earlier Heaven. Or they eat white fungus, thinking that it is the wine of the bodhi. Or they merely sit unmoving, thinking that they are practicing Zen meditation. Or they concentrate on their hearts, thinking that this will cultivate their original nature. It is difficult to enumerate the three thousand six hundred false methods of cultivation, but they all have one common characteristic: they all focus on the physical body. They seek the paths that lead to destruction. Not only can you not achieve immortality through these methods, but when your last breath of yang disappears and your form disintegrates, your spirit will forever sink into the abyss.

The sages say:

The immortal emerges in the One Breath of nothingness,
Empty your body of forms and you will see the original nature.
When your cultivation is complete the pill will descend,
Then you will transcend the mortal realm, become a sage, and journey to the plane of the immortals.

This method is incredible beyond imagination,
It has no beginning, no end, and no form.
If you can intuitively realize its real nature,
Then you will transcend the mortal plane and leave the world behind.

When there is no heart, no things, and no body,
You will meet the possessor of your Earlier Heaven body.
There is only one thing left behind:
The red dust that accumulates below the spiritual altar.

II

EMPTINESS

虛空圖

外而形空
○天空
空無所空

內而心空
○人空
無無所無

遠而物空
○地空
寂無所寂

虛空品十一

Regard the Void and it is empty. In emptiness there is no emptiness. In emptiness there is nothing. In nothingness there is nothing. Since there is nothing in nothingness, there is always stillness. In absolute stillness how can desire arise? When craving does not arise this is true stillness.

Commentary

True emptiness exists when the mind is clear and all forms have disappeared. Externally, there are no objects. Internally, there is no mind. There is only emptiness. In this state, even emptiness does not exist. In true emptiness there is no space, no desire, no will; there are no appearances, no thoughts. All realms of existence are dissolved. In absolute stillness there is no self and no other. There is only Earlier Heaven in its undifferentiated whole.

When there is no desire, one enters a state of true stillness.

The Three Flowers will hover around the crown of the head. The Five Vapors will move toward the Origin. When there is true emptiness in the Lower Burning Space, the lead flower will blossom in the generative energy. When there is true emptiness in the Middle Burning Space the silver flower will blossom in the vital energy. When there is true emptiness in the Upper Burning Space, the golden flower will blossom in the spiritual energy. This is the gathering of the Three Flowers in the cauldron. In emptiness the spirit is still. When you are emptied of happiness, the spirit will be still. When the spirit is still, vapor of the Green Emperor of the East will gather in the direction of the Origin. When you are emptied of anger, the soul is still. When the soul is still, the vapor of the White Emperor of the West will gather in the direction of the Origin. When you are emptied of sorrow, the spiritual energy is still. When the spiritual energy is still, the vapor of the Red Emperor of the South will gather in the direction of the Origin. When you are emptied of happiness, generative energy is still. When generative energy is still, the vapor of the Black Emperor of the North will gather in the direction of the Origin. When you are emptied of desire, then intention is still. When the intention is still, the vapor of the Yellow Emperor in the Center will gather in the direction of the Origin. This is what is meant by the gathering of the five vapors at the origin.

The Confucian sages say, "When desire ceases, the way of heaven can flow." The Buddhists say, "No mind is clear mind." The Taoists say, "Empty the heart and fill the belly." All are referring to the ways of regarding emptiness. Regarding emptiness is not just merely sitting still and stopping thinking. If you do not receive instructions from an enlightened teacher, you will not know how to set up the stove and erect the cauldron. You will not know how to build the foundation, how to gather the herbs, how to obtain the cinnabar, or how to pick the herbs at the right moment. You will not know what is the waterwheel, what is the right amount of fire, what is the union of ch'ien and k'un, what is the interaction of k'an and li, and what is the exchange of metal and wood. You will not know what is meant by the attraction of lead and mercury, what is the rising of yang fire and the falling of yin, what is bathing in stillness, what is the filling of ch'ien and k'un, and what is the sequence of events leading to the emergence of the spirit from the womb.

If you merely sit in stillness, you will not be able to gather the Three Flowers in the cauldron nor direct the Five Vapors toward the Origin. You will wither like dry wood. Your heart will dissolve like ashes. One day your life will be over and you will become a ghost. You may receive offerings and incense or you may be reincarnated as a person of high rank. If you abandon your original nature in this lifetime, all your works in the previous lifetimes will come to nothing.

The sages say:

Riches, fame, and fortune are like dirty water;
See through the illusions and practice in the precious cauldron of emptiness.

Emptiness in form, emptiness in appearance, emptiness in the realm of immortality;
Emptiness in stillness, emptiness in the heart, emptiness in the ruler of human nature;
Emptiness in the principle of emptiness;
Emptiness in appearances and in the senses;
In true emptiness you will see the mysterious workings of heaven.

The way of nonaction is the way of emptiness,
It is not the way of nonconstructive meditation and cultivation of immortal ghost-spirits.

If you receive the teachings from an enlightened teacher,
Without a trace and without a sound the precious pearl will be born.

Translator's Notes

1. The Three Flowers are generative, vital, and spirit energy. Each energy is purified, transmuted, tempered, and stored in the lower, middle, and upper tan-t'ien respectively. The emergence of each flower indicates the completion of a stage of transmutation in the internal alchemical process.

2. The Five Vapors are internal energy stored in the five viscera: the heart, liver, spleen, lungs, and kidneys. Vapor is purified vital energy. The movement of vapor in the five viscera is the "washing" of the internal organs with vital energy. It indicates the completion of the transmutation of generative energy into vital energy and the subsequent movement of vital energy into the internal organs. The organs are first cleansed and then vital energy is stored in them.

12

STILLNESS *and* ORIGINAL NATURE

眞常品十二

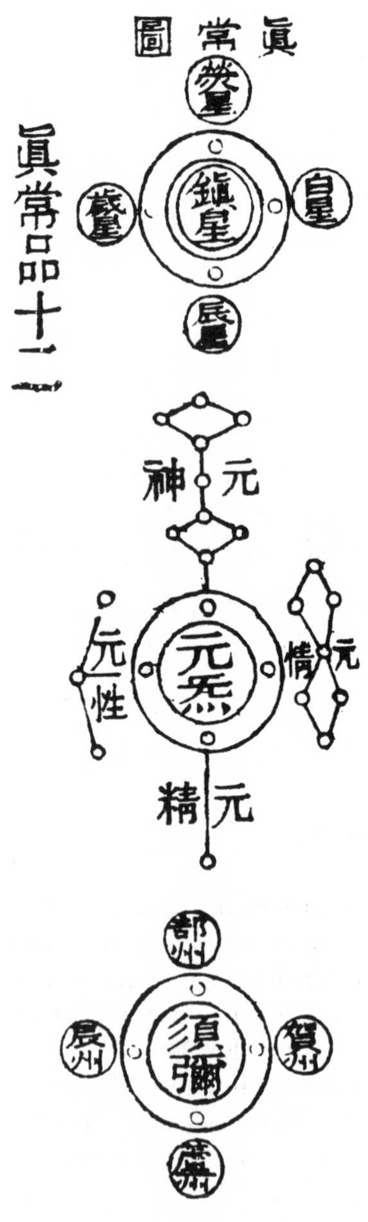

Original nature can intuit all happenings. In original nature is the essence of goodness. Be natural in your actions and you will always be pure and still.

Commentary

In original nature there is no disturbance and no thoughts. In original nature are the five virtues and Five Original Essences. When the spirit is not contaminated this is true nature. To be natural is to act appropriately. When events arise, react to them naturally. When they are gone, return to stillness. This stillness is inaction. Those who practice the Way of the Tao cultivate the pill every day and rid the heart of forms and appearances. They abandon insincerity and hold on to truthfulness.

When yang reaches its zenith, yin is born. When you are absolutely still, everything is at rest. When yin reaches its zenith, yang is born. When pure yang emerges, your intuition will pierce through all that is impermanent. All meridians will flow toward the Origin, and the five virtues of Earlier Heaven will emerge.

In original nature there is goodness. The Five Original Essences emerge through intuition. Intuition is the ability to act naturally in goodness. When the mortal mind is dead, the mind of Tao can live. The One Breath of Earlier Heaven gives us intuition. In intuition is the virtue of humility. When the mind of Tao lives, no thoughts can arise. When no thoughts arise, one returns to Earlier Heaven. In intuition herbs can grow. When the herbs grow, original nature is felt. When original nature is felt, one can act naturally and be natural in response to whatever happens. When one is natural in action, then the waterwheel can turn. When the waterwheel turns, the waters of the sea will flow. When the waters of the sea flow, the fires will be stoked. When the fires are stoked, the golden pill will be born. Therefore, you must always immerse yourself in stillness. If you immerse yourself in stillness, then the original body will form. When the original body is formed, then you will exist as if there is nothing.

People read the *Four Books* and the *Five Classics* and want to be free of desire. However, they only pursue this objective and forget to cultivate their heart and hold on to the original nature. In Buddhism, many practice quiet sitting and imitate the Buddha. They think that the *Diamond Sutra* tells them to extinguish their thoughts and only pursue this objective. They forget to look into the mind and empty it. They do not clear the mind so they can see original nature. In Taoism, many practitioners try to cultivate the treasures and learn the arts of immortality. They say that the book *Cultivating Stillness* speaks of "regarding emptiness." They pursue this objective and forget to empty their hearts and cultivate their original nature. If you just sit without understanding how can you attain the Tao? How can you know that the Tao is the way of heaven?

From heaven all things are born. All life relies on the sun, moon, stars, wind, clouds, thunder, and rain. The *I Ching* says: "The thunder is that which roars; the wind and rain nurture; sun and moon revolve. These are embodied in the seasonal change of winter and summer."

The sages say:

Heaven and earth, sun and moon, have no mind,
The red vapor spreads everywhere and is in every spirit,
The source of all things is with t'ai-chi,
In its natural course harmony is created.
It flows through a thousand and ten thousand years,
It combines the pure and is always supremely pure,
Purity is akin to yang and is resident mysteriously in many virtues,
It is always in cyclical motion and it never ceases.

The breath of the natural course can envelop the universe,
It radiates the first yang and forever permeates through the ages,
Peacefulness and bliss know no boundary,
The pure air emerges from the spirit like the opening of a precious book,
As heaven and earth have their origins, so will this be,
True nature is mysterious through and through.

Translator's Notes

1. The waterwheel turns the waters of life, the internal energy. In the cultivation of the body, this refers to directing the generative energy (ching), which is associated with water, to the head instead of letting it flow out of the body. One waterwheel is at the wei-lu, the interface of the tu and jen meridians. The other waterwheel is the Microcosmic Orbit itself, sometimes also called the Wheel of Life. The waterwheel at the wei-lu is the generator that directs the flow. The Microcosmic Orbit is the wheel that turns in the direction determined by the wheel at the wei-lu. There are three possible directions of flow in the Microcosmic Orbit. One direction is clockwise: the flow is up the tu meridian at the back and down the jen meridian in the front. In this flow is the transmutation of generative energy into vital energy and the transmutation of vital energy into spiritual energy. This returns the ching, or the life energy, to the head. The second direction of flow is counterclockwise: the flow is up the jen meridian and down the tu meridian. In this flow is creation and nourishment of vital energy by spiritual energy and of generative energy by vital energy. The third possible direction is letting the energy flow out of the body. This is leakage. Leakage can occur through the senses and orifices (openings) of the body (eyes, ear, mouth, nose, genital area, and the anus). General constitutional weakness, injury, or craving can all cause leakage.

2. The waters of the sea refer to the energies stored in the Sea of Ch'i. See note 2 in chapter 5 for a discussion of the Sea of Ch'i and related concepts.

3. The fire is the fire of the stove (the lower tan-t'ien). This is the fire that tempers and purifies the generative, vital, and spirit energy.

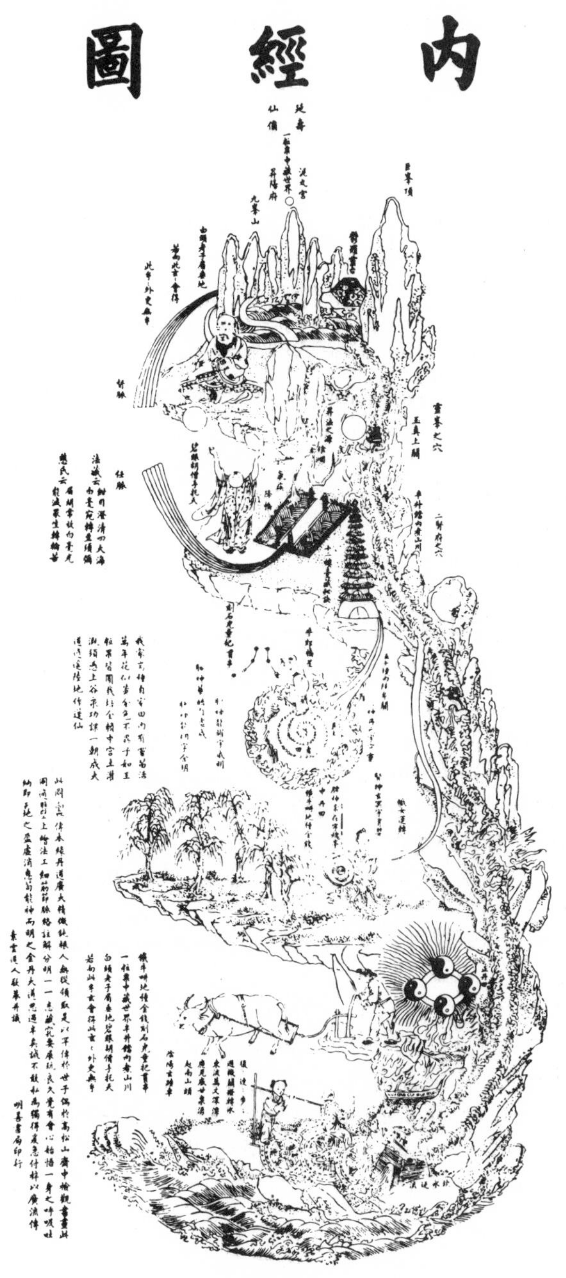

Figure 4.

The picture of the internals, from a woodblock carved during the Ch'ing dynasty, showing the tan-t'iens, the waterwheels, and the fires.

13

The TRUE WAY

眞道圖

眞道品十三

先天 乾卦

後天 離卦

太初

太素　太極　太始

太易

Abide in stillness and you will gradually enter the true way. When you enter the true way, this is called receiving the Tao.

Commentary

In stillness and inaction, we return to Earlier Heaven. When we return to Earlier Heaven, we gradually enter the true way. This is not the three thousand six hundred incorrect paths or the ninety-six digressions. This is the way of Earlier Heaven. From Tao comes heaven, earth, humanity, and all things. The Tao embodies all things. It is wu-chi, the limitless. From old, the teachings of the Tao have been transmitted orally and not committed to writing. The sages were afraid that the writings might fall into the hands of dishonorable people and bring down wrath from heaven. Therefore, although books were written, what was written was encoded in symbolism. As with a tree, the roots are hidden and only the branches are visible. This is the way the teachings of the Tao are expressed.

In our newborn body is the true way. In the union of the seminal fluid of the father and the blood of the mother, lead and mercury combine. Generative energy is lead and blood is mercury. When lead envelops mercury, the essence of ch'ien (male) is born. When mercury envelops lead, the essence of k'un (female) is born. In the first half of the first month yang emerges. In the second half, yin emerges. From there come the five viscera and the six bowels. From there arise the three hundred and sixty-five joints and the eighty-four thousand pores of the body. When Earlier Heaven has run its course, it descends to the mortal realm like an infant tumbling headfirst from the mother's womb. With its first cry the sealed enclosure of Earlier Heaven is broken. The original spirit, original generative force, and original breath emerge from the wu-chi and are divided into three separate entities. In the pa-k'ua, ch'ien loses the middle yang as it descends to k'un. K'un loses its middle yin as it is attracted to ch'ien. The pa-k'ua of Earlier Heaven changes to the pa-k'ua of Later Heaven as the positions of ch'ien and k'un change to li and k'an. From then on water and fire do not mix. This is the existence of Later Heaven, the way of the mortal being.

If you meet with the right teacher, then you are able to return to the true way. The true way begins with pointing to the opening of wu-chi. To the Confucian sages, this opening is called the Original Nature of Goodness. To the Buddhists, it is called nirvana. To the Taoists, it is called the Mysterious Gate. You must use the method of the Concentration of the Six Spirits to hold this opening still. With time, the original spirit will return to its proper place. Next you must use the method of the nine connections called the Nine Circulations of the Golden Pill to transform the pa-k'ua in such a way that li and k'an are repaired. You must take in the vapor of heaven and earth and receive the essence of the sun and moon. Use the strong and mild fires to cultivate the eight treasures of the golden pill and in due time the precious fetus will form. When you have accumulated the three thousand good deeds and fulfilled the eight hundred fruits of labor, the command from heaven will arrive and you will ascend to immortality. You will live in bliss, transcending the mortal plane. No karma will affect you. This is known as the indestructible body of gold. Indeed, you will not be born in vain. To actualize these achievements, you must be taught by an enlightened teacher and you must swear an oath of life and death that you will not stray from the path.

The sages say:

The book of *Cultivating Stillness* is about naturalness,
Intuitively understand the true way,
When you receive the golden pill
You will become an immortal and exist in bliss.

The words in the book *Cultivating Stillness* are not many,
Its meanings are mysterious and few can understand,
This body has the elixir of immortality,
Have you drunk of it before?

In pure stillness in the hour of tzu,
View the clear moon reflected in the river,
This is where you must search for the true way,
Do you understand or not?

Translator's Notes

1. The Nine Circulations of the Golden Pill describes the circular and spiral motion of the internal energy in the body. The golden pill is the culmination of the purification of the generative, vital, and spirit energy. It is also the immortal fetus, the seed of the spirit god. After the immortal fetus is conceived, the spiritual embryo develops and matures. It tumbles around in the tan-t'ien, spiraling and turning like a fetus in the mother's womb. Simultaneously, the internal energy stored in various parts of the body circulates to provide nourishment for the fetus. The movement of the energy also has a spiral quality. In the Macrocosmic Orbit, it travels from the Bubbling Spring at the bottom of the feet to the ni-wan cavity in the head and down again. Nine is the number of completion, and nine also describes the cycle and the period of time required for the energy to complete one circuit. (The minor cycle takes three hours plus three quarter-hours to complete and the major cycle takes nine hours plus nine quarter-hours to complete.) The *Tsan-tung Chi (Triplex Unity)* says that "the method of the Nine Circulations and the emergence of the golden pill is the mystery of the universe. It is sought after by both gods and evil spirits. That is why sages have only transmitted such teachings orally and have refrained from committing this knowledge to writing."

2. The Six Spirits are the spirit energy in six internal organs: the liver, heart, spleen, lungs, kidneys, and gall bladder. The spirit of the liver is known as the mist of the dragon. It is responsible for the clarity of the senses. The spirit of the heart is known as the primordial pill. It gathers the spirit energy. The spirit of the spleen is known as the external existence. It is the protector of the soul. The spirit of the lungs is known as the glorious wonder. It maintains space in the body for energy to circulate. The spirit of the kidneys is known as the great mystery. It nourishes the immortal fetus. The spirit of the gall bladder is known as the brilliant dragon. It is responsible for the force of breath in inhalation and exhalation.

14

The Mysterious Achievement

妙有圖

妙有品十四

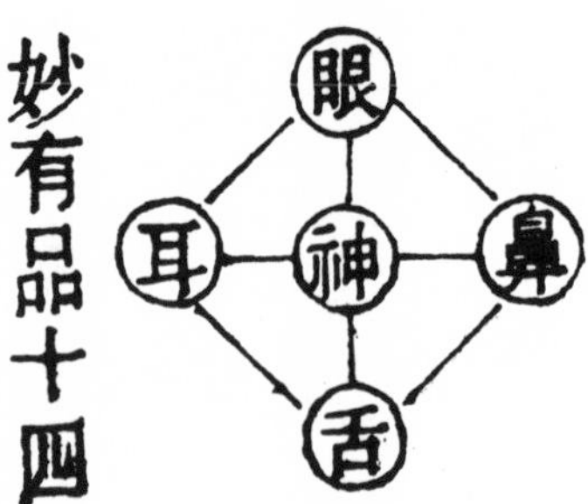

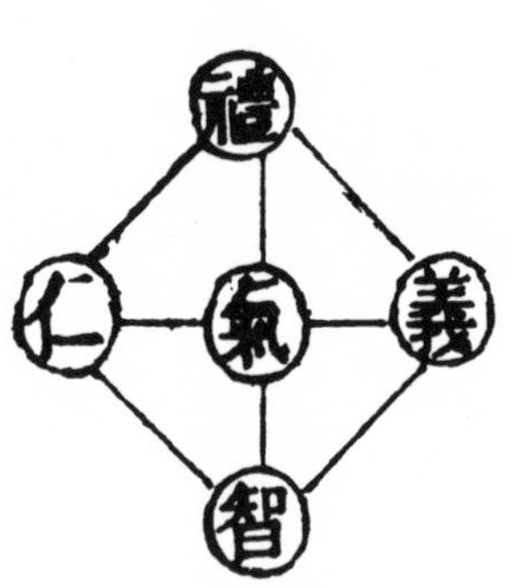

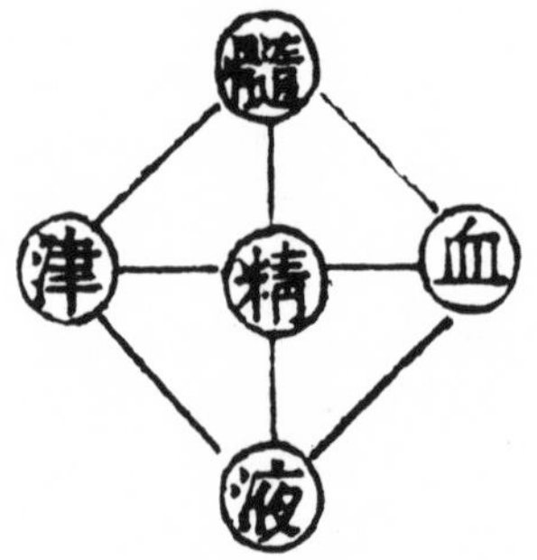

Although we speak of attaining the Tao, there is really nothing to attain.

Commentary

Attaining the Tao means entering the true way and obtaining instructions from an enlightened teacher. Learn the meaning of the Singular Cavity of the Mysterious Gate, the gathering of the Six Spirits, building the foundations, gathering the ingredients to cultivate the pill. Recognize whether the herbs are ready. Get rid of the impurities and retain the pure. Know the meaning of the attraction of mercury and lead and the conception of the fetus. Recognize the Yellow Woman as the go-between. Know how to bring about the interaction of metal and wood, the union of water and fire, the constant turning of the Dharmic Wheel, and the waxing of yang and waning of yin. Learn what are the strong and mild fires and know how to bathe in pure stillness, completing ch'ien and k'un. Know the meaning of the emergence of the infant and the Return of Seven and the Circulation of the Nine. Learn how to change the positions of the stove and cauldron. Know the cry of the dragon and roar of the tiger. Learn to face the wall to cultivate the spirit. Only if you obtain these instructions will you receive the Tao.

Although it is said that you attain the Tao, you are really receiving nothing at all. The Mysterious Gate, the Singular Cavity, and all the treasures described are in the body and not anywhere else. That is why it is said that you receive nothing; you possess them from the beginning. If you want to attain the Tao, you must train and discipline yourself. You must be steadfast like stone and iron, and you must not waiver. Do not crave riches. Do not crave sexual pleasure. Do not be daunted by threats and fear. Your will must be centered, or you will abandon the path along the way. You must isolate your body from fame, fortune, possessive love, liquor, sexual pleasure, and emotions. You must cut them off with a sharp knife. You must cultivate yourself from within. Then you will receive the Tao.

Everyone knows the "external" methods of preserving the body. Those who know the "internal" methods are rare. When you bow before the Golden Cavity and you enjoy the fruits of an immortal lord, then you are truly making a name for yourself. When the golden pill is formed, this precious jewel is true fortune. You have now paid the debt you owed to your parents. This is true filial gratitude. When k'an (water) and li (fire) unite, when metal and wood combine, this is true love. The sweet nectar of the elixir and the fragrance of the bodhi tree are the true wine. The meeting of the immortal fetus and the Fair Maiden in the Yellow Palace is true sexual pleasure. The Seven Treasures of the Jade Pool and the Eight Treasures of the Golden Pill are your real riches. Harmony with the universe and floating on the gentle wind will be your true pleasures.

Lose the external and gain the internal. Abandon the false and gain the real. Train externally and do good works. Cultivate internally and gather the fruits. Be active in helping others to transcend the mortal world. Be still in your efforts to transcend your mortality. Be patient as the sun and moon. Accumulate external deeds and the internal fruits will blossom. When you shed your shell you will ascend to heaven and escape ten thousand kalpas. This is called attaining the Tao, completing the Tao, and extinguishing in the Tao. All these accomplishments can be achieved by those with great vision.

The sages say:

Persuade mortal beings to hope to become sages,
Distance fame, riches, and fortune from your body,
In your body is the wine of immortality,
Let there be nothing in your body that craves riches,
For form is emptiness and emptiness is form,
Immortality is in your original nature and true nature is immortal,
May the world listen to my pleas,
Hurry and embark on the dharma ship.

Mortals should hurry and learn the ways of immortality,
Do not crave liquor and sexual pleasure,
Abandon the false and cultivate the real for the real is not false,
Clear the evil and your way will not be evil,

If you want to heat the pill you must capture the bird in the mountain,
If you want to cultivate the mercury you must capture the frog in the well,
If you can combine these mysterious methods and principles,
Then the mortal can ascend to the heights of the clouds.

Translator's Notes

1. The Yellow Woman is the element earth that occupies the center of the four directions. It is called the go-between because it harmonizes the opposites water and fire in the north-south axis and wood and metal in the east-west axis.

2. The Seven Treasures of the Jade Pool are the seven fluids of life in the body: the fluid of the heart, the liver, the spleen, the lungs, the kidneys, the breath, and the blood.

3. The Return of Seven is the recovery of the seven fluids of life in the body. The seven fluids are in their uncontaminated state when we are born. The fluids become corrupted through aging. The recovery of the fluids is the transformation of the fluids from their contaminated state to their pristine state, as they once were in the body of an infant.

4. The Eight Treasures of the Golden Pill are also known as the Eight Pearls. The Eight Pearls are the essence of life. We were endowed with eight gems of life energy when we were born. After puberty, at age sixteen, one pearl is lost every eight years. When all the pearls are gone, life is over. The Taoist alchemical work is sometimes described as the recovery of the Eight Treasures or the Eight Pearls of Life.

15

The Sacred Path

聖道品十五

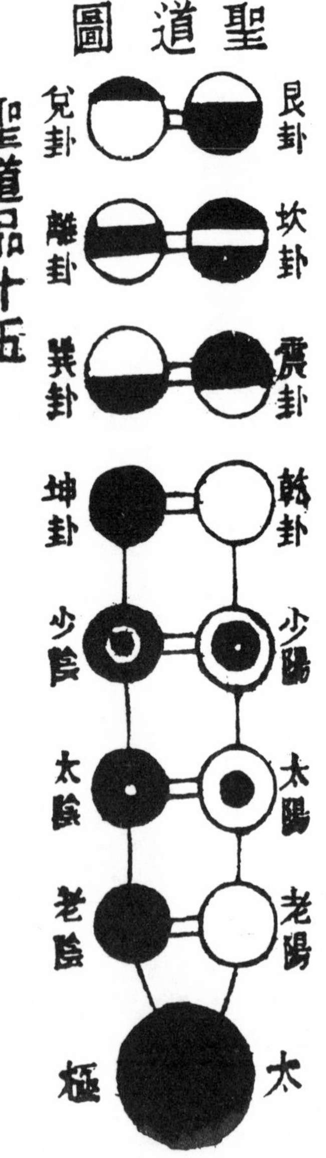

Help all sentient beings. This is attaining the Tao. Those who understand may transmit the teachings of the true way.

Commentary

Help sentient beings to transcend the suffering of the mortal world. Those who understand the teachings live the principles of the Tao by their example, tirelessly teach others, and work hard to accumulate good deeds externally and internally. These people can become teachers who will transmit the principles of the true way. The teachings come from the highest heavenly secrets. When you have accumulated enough good deeds, the Guardians of the Tao will allow you to transmit the teachings.

This is the Third Age of the Teachings and the responsibility for the transmission of the teachings falls on humanity. Immortal Lü says: "A mortal must transcend the realm of mortality and a dragon must penetrate through the mud. Before you receive the permission from heaven, you cannot transmit the teachings of the Tao."

The Confucian sages say: "Heed the way of heaven, heed the great beings, heed the words of the sages." What is the Sacred Path? It concerns your coming into the world. After the union of father and mother, during the first month of pregnancy, wu-chi is formed. In the first half of the month, yang emerges and in the second half of the month yin emerges. In the first half of the second month of pregnancy, wu-chi moves and the yang aspect of wang-chi is formed. In the next half month, wu-chi is still and the yin aspect of wang-chi is formed. In the first half of the third month, wang-chi moves and the yang aspect of t'ai-chi is formed. In the second half of the month, wang-chi reaches its still point and the yin aspect of t'ai-chi is formed. In the first half of the fourth month, t'ai-chi moves and the ancient yang is formed. In the second half of the month, t'ai-chi is still and the ancient yin is formed. In the first half of the fifth month, the ancient yang moves and the greater yang is formed. In the second half of the month, the ancient yin is still and the greater yin is formed. In the first half of the sixth month, the ancient yang is still and the lesser yin is formed. In the second half of the sixth month, the ancient yin is active and lesser yang is formed. In the first half of the seventh month, the greater yang moves, and ch'ien (heaven) is formed. In the second half of the seventh month, the greater yin is still and k'un (earth) is formed. In the first half of the eighth month, the greater yang is still and *tui* (lake) is formed. In the second half of the eight month, the greater yin moves and *ken* (mountain) is formed. In the first half of the ninth month, lesser yin moves and li (fire) is formed. In the second half of the ninth month, lesser yang is still and k'an (water) is formed. In the first half of the tenth month of pregnancy, lesser yin is still and *chen* (thunder) is formed. In the second half of the tenth month, lesser yang moves and *sun* (wind) is formed.

From wu-chi comes wang-chi. From wang-chi comes t'ai-chi, yin and yang, the four directions, the pa-k'ua, and all things, including the three hundred and sixty-five joints in the body, and the eighty-four thousand pores in the skin. All these come through the sacred path from the wu-chi.

The sages say:

Know the way you come and know the way to return,
Do nothing and abide in inaction,
The Origin lies hidden deep and mysterious,
Whether you will be a mortal or a sage depends on it.

If you can, spread the teachings of the Sacred Path and lead the way of compassion,
Help the lost souls to cultivate the light of the original nature,
If you understand the pure stillness of Earlier Heaven,
You will become a golden immortal and live in longevity.

If the sacred path is not taught then the dharma is held back,
Help men and women to overcome the hardships of the mortal world,
Cultivate the five elements, the four perspectives,
And on your head will be the golden crown that flies you to the nine heavens.

TABLE 2.

Wu-chi	formed	first month
	yang emerges	first half of the first month
	yin emerges	second half of the first month
Wu-chi	in movement generates yang in wang-chi	first half of the second month
	in stillness generates yin in wang-chi	second half of the second month
Wang-chi	in movement generates yang in t'ai-chi	first half of the third month
	in stillness generates yin in t'ai-chi	second half of the third month
T'ai-chi	in movement generates the ancient yang	first half of the fourth month
	in stillness generates the ancient yin	second half of the fourth month
Ancient yang	in movement generates the greater yang	first half of the fifth month
Ancient yin	in stillness generates the greater yin	second half of the fifth month
Ancient yang	in stillness generates the lesser yin	first half of the sixth month
Ancient yin	in movement generates the lesser yang	second half of the sixth month
Greater yang	in movement generates ch'ien	first half of the seventh month
Greater yin	in stillness generates k'un	second half of the seventh month
Greater yang	in stillness generates tui	first half of the eighth month
Greater yin	in movement generates ken	second half of the eighth month
Lesser yin	in movement generates li	first half of the ninth month
Lesser yang	in stillness generates k'an	second half of the ninth month
Lesser yin	in stillness generates chen	first half of the tenth month
Lesser yang	in movement generates sun	second half of the tenth month

The sacred path: The creation of all things from wu-chi.

16

Waxing *and* Waning

消長圖

乾爲天

二十四歲
天風姤
澤天夬
十六歲足矣

三十二
天山遯
雷天大壯
十三歲四

四十歲
天地否
地天泰
十歲八月

四十八
風地觀
地澤臨
八歲整

五十六
山地剝
地雷復
五歲四月

至六十四歲足
坤爲地
二歲零八箇月

消長品十六

Lao-tzu says: "The honorable ones have nothing to argue. The dishonorable ones like to argue."

Commentary

The honorable person has great knowledge and wisdom. The learning of the dishonorable person is shallow. Those who have nothing to argue are humble and sincere. Those who like to argue are competitive and egoistic. Lao-tzu says that the mind of the honorable person is like the mind of the sage. It embraces heaven and earth and is in harmony with the principles of heaven. It has a smooth cover and expresses itself humbly. It lowers its sharp peaks and hides its corners. Outside it appears round but inside it is square. It acts according to the principles of heaven. Everything it says is in harmony with all beings. Dishonorable persons like to create arguments. Although they value learning, their roots are shallow and their foundations are unstable. They are unable to learn the ways of the sages. Egoistic people are competitive. They indulge in specialized knowledge and want to display their learning and argue constantly about right and wrong.

The honorable person is like the waxing of yang. The dishonorable person is like the waxing of yin. We should all possess the knowledge of the principles of the waxing and waning of yin and yang, of growth, decay, and death. At birth our bodies are soft and supple, like the flexibility of k'un. After nine hundred and sixty days the first change occurs. At two years and eight months the body enters the first yang. K'un changes into fu. At five years and four months the body enters the second yang. Fu changes into lin. At eight years of age the body enters the third yang. Lin changes into t'ai. At ten years and eight months the body enters the fourth yang. T'ai changes into chuang. At thirteen years and four months the body enters the fifth yang. Chuang changes into kuai. At sixteen years of age the body enters the sixth yang. Kuai changes into ch'ien. At this time the body has reached the zenith of health and is purely yang in nature. If you cultivate original mind and body now, you can reach the realm of the immortals and sages. If you do not cultivate your mind and body now, you will gradually degenerate into the dishonorable character. At twenty-four the body enters the first yin. Ch'ien changes into k'ou. If you cultivate original mind and body now, you can still achieve immortality without too much difficulty. If you do not cultivate yourself at this time, the body will reach the second yin at thirty-two. K'ou changes into tun. However, if original nature and body are cultivated now, it is still an easy process. But, if you still neglect to cultivate yourself, the body will enter the third yin at forty years of age. Tun changes into pi. At this point, cultivation of nature and body is still possible. However, if you continue not to cultivate yourself, the body will enter the fourth yin at forty-eight. Pi changes into kuan. At this time you can still cultivate body and mind but results will only occur after long periods of hard work. If you still fail to cultivate yourself, then the body will reach the fifth yin at fifty-six. Kuan changes into po. During this time cultivation of original nature and body is still possible but it will be a very difficult process. If you continue not to cultivate yourself, the body will enter the sixth yin at sixty-four years of age. Po changes into k'un. Now the body is primarily yin in nature. However, at this time you can still take advantage of the last breath of yang in the body. With tremendous effort, you can remove the yin, recover the yang, and escape from death. If you do not cultivate your mind and body at this point, then the last breath of yang will be extinguished and life will be just a dream. Whether you are old or young you must return to the path of life as soon as possible. Do not wait till death to regret that you abandoned the path of immortality during your lifetime.

The sages say:

The honorable one who does not argue has the virtues of the sage.
The three religions (Confucianism, Buddhism, and Taoism) come from the same source.
The Tao is harmonious, mysterious, and without form.
Like the light of the moon in a cloudless sky its light shines over the four seas.
It flows like a thousand rivers and is reflected in heaven, earth, and humankind.
A body full of yang becomes immortal and a body full of yin becomes a ghost.

It is a pity that people these days are ignorant of this
wisdom.

The book *Cultivating Stillness* is filled with wisdom.
The honorable one who does not argue is formless and
elusive.
If your body shines with a bright light,
Then you will believe in the movement of ch'ien and
k'un in the hidden cycles.
Everywhere is the Void concealing the bright full moon.
It shines forever to guide the universe and all beings.
That the dishonorable person argues and the honorable
person concedes is the way of yin and yang.
The sages and virtuous ones can definitely be distinguished.

Translator's Note

See the translator's introduction for a discussion of the hexagrams and the waxing and waning of yang and yin.

17

VIRTUES

道德圖

道德品十七

上德

先天

中道

忠恕 儒 仁義禮智信

慈悲 釋 殺盜淫妄酒

感應 道 金木水火土

下德

後天

凡道

Those who possess high virtues do not need virtue. Those who possess mundane virtues have to force themselves to be virtuous. Those who argue about virtues do not know virtue.

Commentary

High virtues come from Earlier Heaven. In Earlier Heaven all five virtues are complete. Confucianism teaches uprightness, sacrifice, propriety, intelligence, and trust as virtues and regards dedication and forgiveness as moral actions. Buddhism views abstinence from killing, robbery, sexual perversity, madness, and drunkenness as virtues and regards kindness and compassion as moral actions. In Taoism, virtue is the cultivation of the five elements (gold, wood, water, fire, earth) and moral action is intuitive understanding. The highest virtues are untainted because they have not been touched by Later Heaven. Therefore, there is no need to improve on the high virtues. They are originally in us and there is no need to look for them elsewhere.

Those who possess mundane virtues need to make an effort to be virtuous. This is because their virtues are influenced by Later Heaven and are no longer pristine. The essence of the five high virtues is lost. If these people do not make an effort to be virtuous, then it will be very difficult for them to return to Earlier Heaven. They need to know what is wrong and then make an effort to correct it. They must stop killing and recover uprightness; stop unscrupulous actions and recover selflessness; stop sexual perversity and recover propriety; stop drunkenness and regain intelligence; stop rash actions and regain trust. Uprightness, selflessness, propriety, intelligence, and trust need to be achieved by conscious effort.

Those who argue about virtue do not know what is true virtue. They see people refrain from killing and criticize them for placing too much value on animal life at the expense of their health. They see people being kind to the poor and criticize them for emptying their pockets to pay another person's debts. They see people refrain from sexual perversity and criticize them for repressing their desire. They see others refrain from drunkenness and say that meat and wine are for eating and drinking. They see others not speak rashly and say that if the intentions are good, it should not matter what is said. They argue about everything and understand nothing. They do not know what uprightness, selflessness, propriety, intelligence, and trust mean in Confucianism. They do not know what is meant by cultivating gold, wood, water, fire, and earth. They do not know what is meant by abstinence from killing, robbery, perversities, madness, and drunkenness.

If you do not refrain from killing, then you are not upright. The element wood will be missing. In heaven, the ruling star of the year will not be at rest. On earth, there will be disasters in the east. In the body, the liver and the gall bladder will be injured. If you do not refrain from stealing, then you do not have the virtue of selflessness. The element metal will be missing. In heaven, the star *T'ai-pa* (the White Tiger) will not be at peace. On earth, there will be disasters in the west. In the body, the lungs and the large intestine will be injured. If you indulge in sexual pursuits, in heaven, the star *Yin-h'ua* will not be at rest. On earth, there will be disasters in the south. In the body, the heart and the small intestine will be injured. If you do not refrain from drunkenness, then your intelligence is lost. The element water will be missing. In heaven, the Morning Star will not be at peace. On earth, there will be disasters in the north. In the body, the kidneys and the bladder will be injured. If you do not refrain from madness and rash actions, then the virtue trust will be lost. The element earth will be missing. In heaven, the Guardian Star will not be at rest. On earth, there will be disasters at the center. In the body, the spleen and the stomach will be injured.

The sages say:

The virtues of Earlier Heaven are of pure yang,
If you are willing to cultivate them they will be strong,
If the five virtues, the five centers, and the Three Treasures are complete,
Then what need is there to work hard to hang onto the virtues?

The three religions come from the same origin,
Why is there the need to distinguish east and west,
They are in the Three Flowers, the Three Treasures, and the Three Refuges,

They are in the five virtues, the five elements, and the
five abstinences.

The completion of the virtues is a most mysterious
thing,
It relies on the foundations of the five abstinences.
You who are stubborn and who hold your heads high,
Do not wait until you are in the realm of the dead to
regret,
For then it will be too late.

18

FORGETTING *the* MIND

妄心圖

脾富豪
肺貴顯
心仙壽
肝妻美
腎子孝

妄心品十八

Sentient beings are unable to enter the true way because their minds are untamed.

Commentary

What is "an untamed mind"? In Chinese, the word *untamed* is made up of two components: "forgetting" and "woman." An untamed mind is one that "forgets the woman or the female." The mind belongs to the li position of the pa-k'ua. The trigram (☲) represents fire and sun. The sun is the ruler of the mind (or heart). The female is the symbol of queenliness. She is just and incorruptible. Her light shines on the world and gives life to all. Forgetting the female therefore means forgetting the true nature that is in us.

How does the mind become wild? The causes are liquor, sex, riches, anger, frustration, fame, fortune, passion, and possessive love. People desire liquor to gratify the body momentarily and do not know the harm that it can bring. It confuses the mind and blots out original nature. The meridians of the human body parallel the movement of the celestial bodies of heaven. The internal energy circulates as the bodies of heaven move through the skies. When you drink alcohol, the energy's passage through the meridians becomes disordered. When the energy's movement is disordered, the constellations in the human body are disturbed. As the constellations in the body are disturbed, the life span is shortened.

People desire sex to gratify the body and do not know the harm that sexual activity can bring. In the human body, the generative force (ching) is used to cultivate vital energy (ch'i), and the vital energy is used to cultivate the spirit (shen). Only by possessing these Three Treasures can you have a long life. If you crave sex, then the generative energy will be dissipated. Consequently, vital energy cannot be cultivated, and the spirit cannot develop. As the Three Treasures are depleted, the life span will shorten.

People crave riches and do not know the harm that is caused by focusing on obtaining riches. The energy that is used to cultivate the Three Treasures is spent on getting material goods. Even if you have millions you cannot buy the health and life that you have lost. When you die, you leave empty-handed, only to return to the wheel of suffering.

People cannot control their anger and frustration. They do not know the harm that is caused by the inability to calm their feelings. When you cannot control anger and frustration, that which is trivial is blown out of proportion. You worry needlessly over the family fortune, whether you will get into trouble with the government, whether your spouse or your children will desert you.

People want to make a name for themselves and gratify

their desire for fame. They do not know the harm that is caused by fame. Try to make a name for yourself in the arts and letters and you will overwork your mind. Try to make a name for yourself in the military and martial arts and you will overwork your body. You spend your life overworking yourself, and, even if you achieve a high rank in your profession, you will not have the health to enjoy it. If you are honest and dedicated, then when you die, you may become a guardian spirit. If you are cruel and evil you will fall into endless suffering through reincarnations.

People desire possessive love to gratify their desire to be loved. They do not know the harm that possessive love can cause. When you have money and fortune, your spouse is loyal and the children are filial. If you lose your fortune, your spouse will be unfaithful and your children will not be filial. Many honest people have been lured into the false security of possessive love, thinking that it means having a faithful spouse and filial children. When you die, you cannot take your spouse and children with you.

Be aware of the ephemeral nature of material things. Lose your attachment to them. If you do not pursue the path of immortality and seek the true way, how can you become an enlightened being?

The sages say:

Abandon the wild and untamed ways and become a sage,
Riches, fame, and fortune are like floating clouds,
Know that what you have is the work of previous karma,
Why spend your life injuring your body and spirit?

When the true nature does not dissipate,
This is called returning to the center,
There are no signs and no forms,

There is only emptiness,
Leave the untamed heart and regain the Way,
These golden words of teaching are very difficult to encounter.

Wash away the dirt of the heart and learn the way of the Buddha,
Have no thoughts, no desire, and live without stress,
Do not be involved in liquor, sex, riches, and negative emotions,
Learn the art of longevity and your years will number ten thousand.

19

The SPIRIT

人神圖

風

火

地

水

人神品十九

When the mind is wild, the spirit is distracted.

Commentary

A wild or untamed mind is always in motion. The mind is the residence of the spirit. The spirit is the ruler of all actions and thoughts. Those who engage in Taoist training must not let the mind run wild because when the mind is not still, the spirit is distracted. The spirit is hidden in the mind. It is the essence of Earlier Heaven. The spirit of heaven resides in the sun. In the human body the spirit manifests itself in the eyes. The mind is the ruler of the spirit. The eyes are the point where the spirit is gathered. There are sixty-four guardian gods resident in sixty-four locations in the body, reflected in the sixty-four trigrams of the *I Ching*. During conception, wu-chi is formed. From wu-chi emerges wang-chi, t'ai-chi, the two opposites (yin and yang), the four directions, and the pa-k'ua. The parts of the human body emerge with the differentiation of the One into many. This is the earthly path of mortality. In the return to the Origin, the parts of the body return to the sixty-four trigrams; the sixty-four trigrams return to the Sixteen Rulers; the Sixteen Rulers return to the pa-k'ua; the pa-k'ua returns to the four directions; the four directions return to yin and yang, and finally yin and yang return to t'ai-chi and wu-chi.

If you want to return to the Origin, every day you must maintain stillness and not let the spirit be distracted. When the spirit is not distracted, then the sixty-four guardian gods will gather toward the spirit. When the spirit is in union with the sixty-four guardian gods, then its light will be radiant and strong. If its light is strong, original nature will shine. This is the path of immortality.

If you obtain the method of the Circulation of the Nine, then you will be able to cultivate the yang spirit and become the Golden Immortal of the Great Realm. If you obtain the external methods to complement your training, then you will be able to become the Heavenly Immortal of the Great Realm. The Circulation of the Nine must be taught by an enlightened teacher. Then the Sixteen Rulers of the body will radiate the light of spring.

The mind is the sovereign of all. It is the seat of intuition and insight. The radiance of the spirit emanates from it. The eyes are officers who patrol and watch. They guard what is seen. The mouth guards speech and attends to what is spoken. The ears are the officers of hearing. They judge what is heard. The nose guards what is smelled. The liver is the military general. From it comes strategic planning. The lungs are the ministers. From them come responsibility and propriety. The spleen is the ombudsman. From it comes ethical actions and unbiased judgment. The kidneys are lords of strength. From them come skill and power. The gall bladder is the minister of justice. From it comes judgment and decision. The stomach is the officer who guards the food stores. From it comes the regulation of food resources and the five tastes. The middle of the thorax is the officer who regulates the emotions and feelings. The small intestine is the officer of the treasury. It has the riches and resources to feed the nation. The large intestine is the official who propagates the right ways of living. Through it, internal rhythms are kept and changes are effected. The bladder is the officer who oversees the provinces and ensures that the flow of the waters is regulated. The three burning spaces are officers of the waterworks who build ditches, sewers, and sluices so that the waste may be channeled out of the body. These are the sixteen guardian gods. They are the rulers of the body. Of all the sixteen guardian gods, the heart is the sovereign. It gives power to the eyes, ears, nose, and mouth, and appoints them as the four prime ministers. The rest take lower ranks. All the officers and lesser ministers are subordinate to the sovereign.

The sages say:

People fall into the pit of the red dust of the mortal realm,
Because their thoughts run wild and they have forgotten the pure skies,
If you do not obtain the teachings from an enlightened master,
How can you hope to ascend to the realm of immortality?
When the ties to evil deeds are cut, your roots will be pure,

When the six senses are empty, the five elements will be complete,
The Ancient Sage has spoken the golden words,
Heed them and though there exist ten thousand kalpas, you will live in eternity.

When thoughts run wild, the spirit will disintegrate into ten thousand directions,
Your soul will end up in hell and your true yang will be lost,
Snow, frost, and angry waves sweep the levels of hell,
Trees and mountains are like knives that cut mercilessly,
Center your thoughts on the One and return to the springtime,
Let the vapor from the three tan-t'iens flow with fragrance,
Hurry and return to purity and stillness,
Do not waste the time you are allotted on earth.

20

The Myriad World *of* Ten Thousand Things

萬物圖

萬物品二十

天
天
風
月
星
雷
日
雨

When the spirit is distracted, it will attach itself to the ten thousand myriad things.

Commentary

When the spirit is distracted it is not still. When the mind runs wild, the spirit is led astray by knowledge. If it is not thinking of things in heaven, it is thinking about things on earth. If it is not thinking about things on earth, it is thinking of things in the body. However, the phenomena in heaven are but the sun, moon, stars, planets, wind, clouds, thunder, and rain. The things on earth are but mountains, rivers, grass, and trees. They all emerge from the five elements. The things of the world are but fame, fortune, passion, possessive love, liquor, sex, riches, and emotions. The parts of the human body are but the five elements, the pa-k'ua, earth, water, wind, and vastness. All things in heaven, earth, and the human body originate in Earlier Heaven.

The pa-k'ua of Earlier Heaven is arranged in the following way. Ch'ien (heaven) is in the south and k'un (earth) is in the north. Li (fire) is in the east and k'an (water) is in the west. These are four positions of the main axis. Chen (thunder) is in the northeast and sun (wind) is in the southwest. Ken (mountain) is in the northwest and tui (lake) is in the southeast. These are the positions of the off-axis. The three yang components of ch'ien are opposite to the three yin components of k'un. This is called the positioning of heaven and earth. The lower yang component and upper two yin components (☳) in chen are opposite to the lower yin component and upper two components (☴) of yang in sun. This pair is called the complementarity of thunder and wind. The middle yang component and outer two yin components (☵) of k'an are opposite to the inner yin component and outer two yang components (☲) of li. This pair of opposites is the noncompetitiveness of water and fire. The upper yang component and lower two yin components (☶) of ken are opposite to the upper yin component and lower two yang components (☱) of tui. This pair of opposites is described as the flow of air between mountain and lake. These complementary pairs represent the state of affairs of Earlier Heaven.

Earlier Heaven is the path of immortality. Through the process of differentiation, the yang in ch'ien interacts with the yin in k'un and k'un is transformed into k'an. The yin in k'un interacts with the yang in ch'ien and ch'ien is transformed into li. The upper yin component of k'an interacts with the upper yang component of li and li is transformed into chen. The lower yang component of li interacts with the lower yin component of k'an and k'an is transformed into tui. The upper two yin components of chen interact with the upper two yang component of sun and sun is transformed into k'un. The upper yang component and lower yin component of sun interact with the upper yin component and lower yang component of chen. Chen becomes ken. The upper yang component of ken and lower yin component of ken interact with the upper yin component and lower yang component of tui. Tui becomes sun. The lower two yin components of tui interact with the lower two components of ken and ken becomes ch'ien. After these transformations, li is in the south, k'an is in the north, chen is in the east, and tui is in the west. Ch'ien occupies the northwest, sun, the southeast, ken, the northeast, and k'un, the southwest. The pa-k'ua of Earlier Heaven is thus transformed into the pa-k'ua of Later Heaven.

If you do not know the principles of Earlier Heaven, you will not be able to achieve immortality even if you have the methods of training in Later Heaven.

The sages say:

All things originate in one body,
The movements of heaven and earth follow the same principles,
Mortal beings do not know the depth of the Origin,
Their nature falls into hell and their bones are forever buried.

If people can find their beginnings in Earlier Heaven,
They can return to the Origin of the One Emptiness,
When wild thoughts do not arise, you can return to the t'ai-ch'i.
Thunder will rise from the bottom of the sea to reveal the sacred turtle.

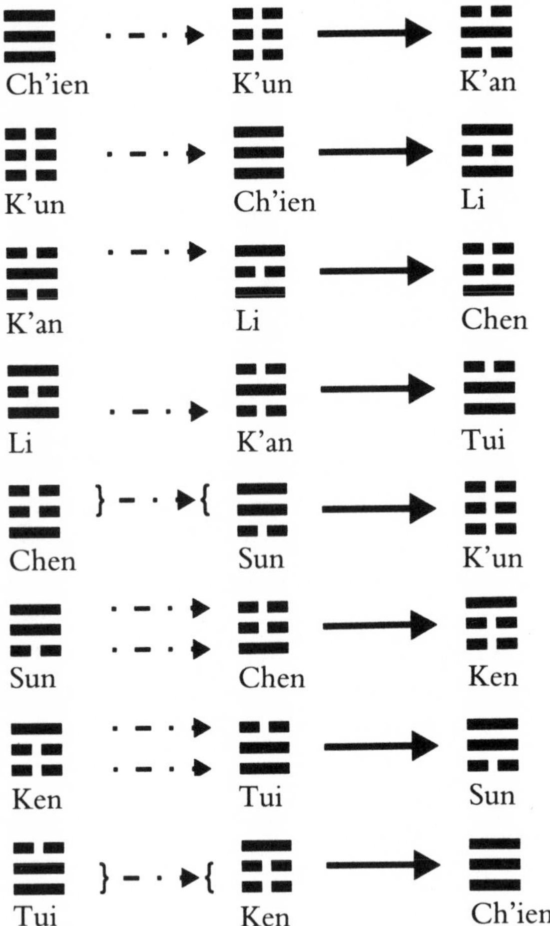

Figure 5.

The transformation of the Earlier Heaven pa-k'ua into the Later Heaven pa-k'ua.

If there are no wild thoughts, the spirit will not be distracted,
Then all things will return to their original purity.
Hurry and find the cavity of the radiant intuition,
Cultivate your nature and recover your heart to become a sage.

21

Craving *and* Desire

貪求圖

貪求品二十一

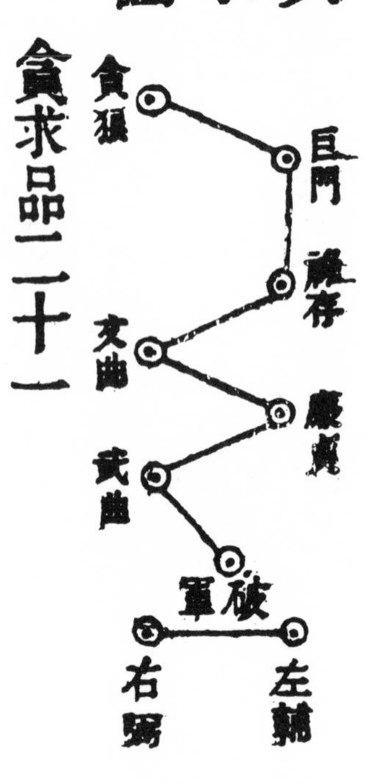

When the ten thousand things arise, craving and desire emerge.

Commentary

When the mind is disturbed, it is attracted by ten thousand things. With attraction, craving will arise. With craving, the desire to obtain things to satisfy craving will emerge. The mind that desires is rooted in earthly existence and is controlled by the pa-k'ua of Later Heaven. When we recover our immortal roots, riches will be seen as floating clouds, liquor and sex will lose their attraction, and Later Heaven will be transformed into Earlier Heaven. Those who can dissolve craving are extraordinary persons. They are one in tens of thousands.

Many people are attached to craving and are controlled by the forces of Later Heaven. Therefore they cannot return to Earlier Heaven. They cannot transform the Lo-shu (Later Heaven pa-k'ua) into the Ho-to (Earlier Heaven pa-k'ua).

The star Craving Wolf is the first star named in the North Star constellation. It symbolizes desire, which is said to resemble wild wolves. Those who cultivate immortality must tame this star in themselves or else they will not attain the Tao. In the Later Heaven pa-k'ua, the numbers two, four, six, eight, and ten are yin in nature. Because they are yin in nature, they generate craving and desire. On earth the number six belongs to the celestial stem kuei and the element water. This element controls the sensations related to the release of the generative force and is manifested in the desire for bodily pleasure and sex. On earth the number two belongs to the celestial stem ting and belongs to the element fire. The element fire controls thoughts related to planning for success and is manifested in the desire for fortune and fame. On earth the number eight belongs to the celestial stem i and the element wood. Wood controls the emotions and is manifested in the craving for riches. On earth the number four belongs to the celestial stem hsin and the element metal. Metal controls cruelty and is manifested in the craving for liquor and luxurious food. On earth the number ten belongs to the celestial stem chi and the element earth. It is the ruler of selfish acts and is manifested in the need to satisfy one's pride and ego. These are the five evils of Later Heaven. They are the enemies of the five elements in the body.

Craving for sex dissipates the generative force (ching) and the element water is harmed. Craving for riches injures original nature and the element wood is harmed. Craving for fame and fortune injures the spirit (shen) and the element fire is harmed. Desire to inflict harm on others injures compassion and the element metal is harmed. Egoism injures the vital

TABLE 3.

TRIGRAM	NUMBER	DIRECTION	ELEMENT	CELESTIAL STEM
k'an water	6 (1)	north	water	kuei (jen)
li fire	2 (7)	south	fire	ting (ping)
chen thunder	8 (3)	east	wood	i (chia)
tui lake	4 (9)	west	metal	hsin (keng)
center	10 (5)	center	earth	chi (wu)

The pa-k'ua, the elements, and the Celestial Stems. Odd numbers are yang numbers. Even numbers are yin numbers. The even and odd numbers correspond to the black circles and white circles in the pa-k'ua as presented in the Lo-shu. The Celestial Stems also have yin and yang components. Kuei, ting, i, hsin, and chi are yin. Jen, ping, chia, keng, and wu are yang.

energy in our body (ch'i) and the element earth is harmed. When the five elements are harmed, the body will become ill.

If you wish to attain immortality you must transform Later Heaven into Earlier Heaven. Let the middle yang component of k'an return to the center of li, transforming li into ch'ien. Let the middle yin component of li return to the center of k'an, thus transforming k'an into k'un. Let the upper yin component of chen return to tui, transforming tui to k'an. Let the lower yang component of tui return to the upper component of chen, transforming chen into li. Let the upper two yang components of ch'ien return to the upper two components of k'un, transforming k'un into sun. Let the lower two yin components of k'un return to the lower two components of ch'ien, transforming k'un into ken. Let the upper yang and lower yin components of ken return to the lower and upper component of sun, transforming sun into tui. Let the upper yang and lower yin components of sun return to the upper and lower components of ken, transforming ken into chen. Let the positions of the pa-k'ua be exchanged such that Later Heaven is transformed into Earlier Heaven. Let the five evils dissolve and be transformed into the five elements. Let the Ho-tu be transformed into the Lo-shu. Those who can achieve this are extraordinary persons.

The sages say:

The mysterious ways of the Ancient One of Most High
Have transmitted to us these precious teachings.
The Three Flowers, the Three Treasures belong to the Origin,
The five thieves and five evil gods belong to Later Heaven.
Relocate the positions of the trigrams and extinguish the fires,
Place the stove and erect the cauldron to cultivate the golden pill.
Live a natural life and do not crave and desire,
One day lived in peace is one day closer to immortality.

Earlier Heaven becomes Later Heaven and Later Heaven can be transformed into Earlier Heaven,
There is a big difference between mortal ways and the way of the sage,
Riches, fame, and fortune are as ephemeral as lightning,
The passion of sexual love and childish piety will vanish like flames.

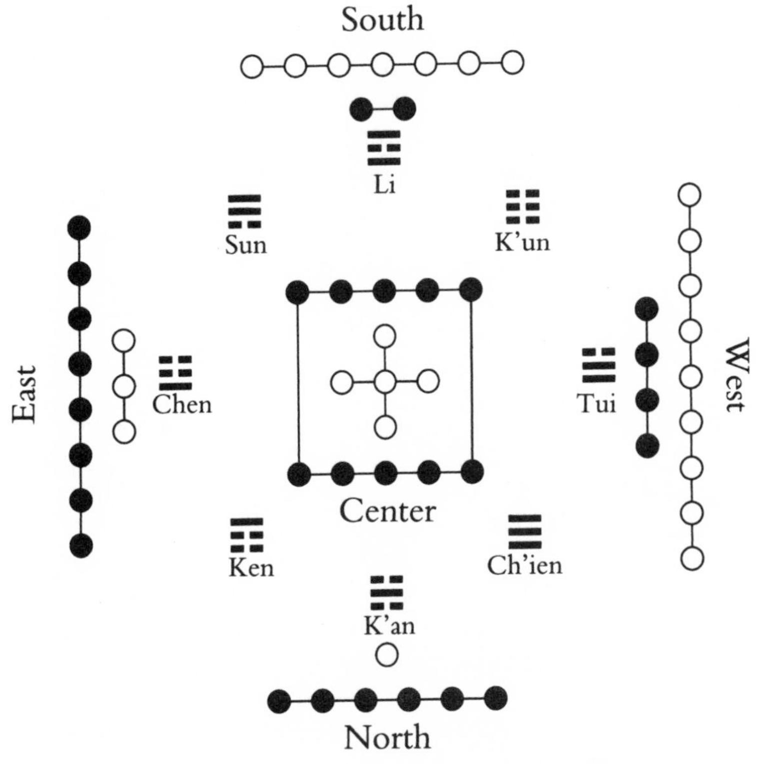

Figure 6.

The pa-k'ua as presented in the Lo-shu. Black circles are yin numbers, and white circles are yang numbers.

Do not crave and be the master of your own life,
Cultivate the Tao and there will be gods to help your karma,
Do not lose your original nature and the dust of the earthly realm will vanish,
The sky will reveal the circular bright moon.

Translator's Notes

1. Each position of a pa-k'ua has a pair of numbers associated with it. (See table 3, page 50.) The odd number is yang and symbolizes creation. The even number is yin and symbolizes completion. The numbers in the north, south, east, west, and center are paired in the following way: north—1, 6; south—2, 7; east—3, 8; west—4, 9; center—5, 10. Therefore, in each position is creation and completion, yang and yin. The *I Ching* says, "The One of Heaven creates water in the north and the Six of Earth completes it. The Three of Heaven creates wood in the east and the Eight of Earth completes it. The Five of Heaven creates earth in the center and the Ten of Earth completes it. The Seven of Heaven creates fire in the south and the Two of Earth completes it. The Nine of Heaven creates metal in the west and the Four of Earth completes it." The complementariness of yin and yang (creation and completion) generates all things. See also note 1 in chapter 8.

2. See note 1 in chapter 8 for a discussion of the Celestial Stems.

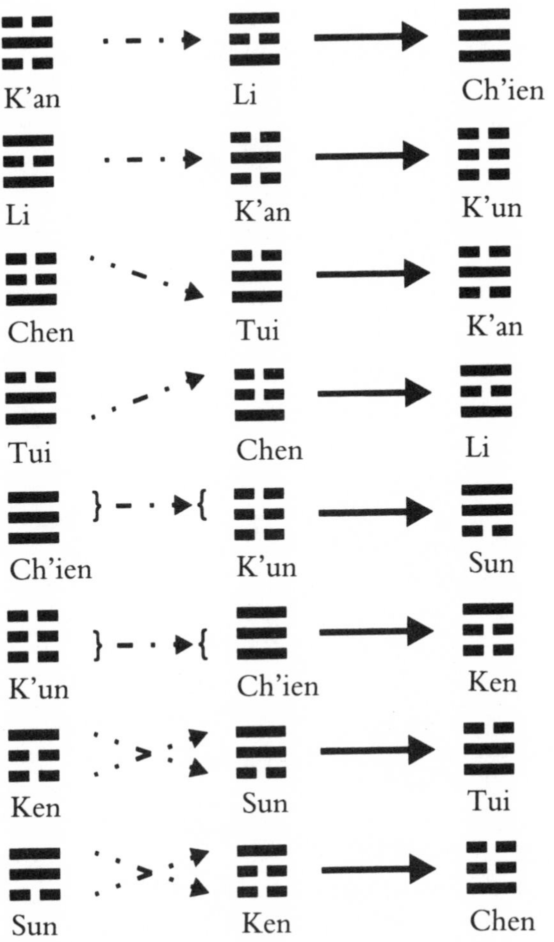

Figure 7.

The transformation of the Later Heaven pa-k'ua into the Earlier Heaven pa-k'ua.

22

ANXIETY *and* STRESS

煩惱圖

Because of desire and craving, stress and anxiety arise. Because there are anxiety and stress, body and mind are afflicted by tensions.

Commentary

Anxiety and stress generate worry, irritation, unrest, and tension. The body is form and the mind is the ruler. Because people cannot detach themselves from fame, fortune, passions, possessive love, liquor, sex, and riches, they are imprisoned by the six dusts and the six thieves.

Those who crave fortune and fame but cannot obtain them will develop anxiety and anger. Those who possess fortune and fame will encounter more anxiety and tension because they are afraid of losing them. See through the illusion of fame and fortune and pursue the Tao. When you achieve immortality, then your name will be on records past and present. The *Tao-te Ching* says that one must face the wall, restrain the wild horses, and sit quietly to enter into the Tao.

Those who crave riches but cannot obtain them will develop anxiety and anger. Those who possess riches will encounter more anxiety and tension because they are afraid of losing them. See through the illusion of riches and follow the Tao. The Three Treasures in your body will be your riches. You will live a long life without stress. The sages say, "To me riches are but floating clouds." The *Golden Mean* says, "If you are poor, live in poverty." Mencius says, "Poverty cannot be changed." He also says, "The honorable person is concerned with the Tao and not with poverty."

Those who crave beauty and sexual attractiveness but do not have them will develop anxiety and anger. Those who possess them will encounter more anxiety and tension because they are afraid of losing them. See through the illusion of beauty and sexual attractiveness and cultivate the Tao. When you develop the immortal fetus in your body, when k'an and li interact, metal and wood unite, you will receive the highest reward. You will live forever in the company of immortals. The sages say, "If the blood is stirred, you must abstain from sexual desire." Immortal Lü says, "View beautiful bodies as liquor and use your sword to cut down the fool in yourself. Although you will not see a head fall to the ground, you will learn from this lesson and let your cravings wither."

Those who like to argue will develop anxiety and tension from worrying too much about what is right and what is wrong. See through the illusion of emotions and pursue the Tao. Cultivate the Three Flowers, the Five Vapors, the Breath of Yang, the Universal Breath in your body, and complete the golden pill. The sages say, "If the blood is boiling over, you must learn to abstain from arguments. Center your will and do not show anger."

The sages say:

Do not crave liquor, sex, and riches,
Wealth and poverty are the results of cause and effect,
Form is empty and emptiness is form,
Smoke is the result of flame and from flames arises smoke,
If you worry, then you will be anxious and stressed,
Take the parts from k'an and return them to li,
Sweep away desire, return your thoughts to the One and the realm of dust will vanish,
Cultivate the precious pearl so that it shines like the clear moon.

Do not crave fame, fortune, and sexual pleasure,
Every day lie on your back and look toward the many-colored clouds,
When you are hungry magical monkeys will give you peaches,
When you are thirsty the dragon woman will give you tea,
You far surpass the fortunes of the three thousand families at the mouth of the Han river,
You far outdistance the wealth of the hundred thousand families in the capital city,
Let the mortals of this world hurry and awaken,
Sweep away their anxieties and stress and cut through the yellow grass.

23

LIFE *and* DEATH

生死品二十三

生死圖

河圖生

洛書死

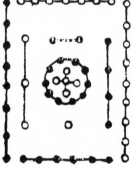

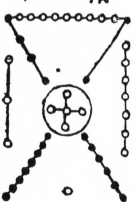

If you live in disappointment and anxiety you will sink into the ocean of suffering and forever stray from the True Way.

Commentary

If you crave riches, fame, fortune, passions, and possessive love, you will develop anxiety, stress, and disappointment. You will fall into the trap of the five impurities and sink forever into endless suffering. Life is symbolized by the Ho-to (Earlier Heaven pa-k'ua) and death by the Lo-shu (Later Heaven pa-k'ua). Those attached to drunkenness, sexual desire, riches, and anger, are wanderers lost on the path of life and death. They do not know from where they came and whence they will go. The way of the mortal is described in the Lo-shu and the way of the immortal is described in the Ho-to.

During conception, the union of the original breath of the father and mother forms a bright pearl called wu-chi. Receiving the generative force of the father and the blood of the mother, the t'ai-chi is formed. In heaven, the number one gives birth to water in jen. In the upper part of the body it forms the opening in the left eye (the pupil) and in the lower part of the body it forms the bladder. On earth, the number two gives birth to the fire of ting. In the upper part of the body it forms the right eye and in the lower part of the body it forms the heart. In heaven, the number three gives birth to wood in chia. In the upper part of the body it forms the black pearl of the left eye (the iris) and in the lower part of the body it forms the gall bladder. On earth, the number four gives birth to metal in hsin. In the upper part of the body it forms the white pearl in the right eye (the sclera) and in the lower part of the body it forms the lungs. In heaven, the number five gives birth to earth in wu. In the upper part of the body it forms the left eyelid. In the lower part of the body it forms the stomach. On earth, the number six gives form to water in kuei. In the upper part of the body it forms the opening of the right eye (the pupil). In the lower part of the body it forms the kidneys. In heaven, the number seven gives form to fire in ping. In the upper part of the body it forms the boundary of the left eye. In the lower part of the body it forms the small intestine. On earth, the number eight gives form to wood in i. In the upper part of the body it forms the black pearl (the iris) of the right eye. In the lower part of the body it forms the liver. In heaven, the number nine gives form to metal in keng. In the upper part of the body it forms the white part of the left eye (the sclera). In the lower part of the body it forms the large intestine. On earth, the number ten gives form to earth in chi. In the upper part of the body it forms the right eyelid. In the lower part of the body it forms the spleen. Thus, the five viscera, the six bowels, the three hundred and sixty-five joints of the body, and the eighty-four thousand pores in the skin are formed from the design and development of the Ho-to. Sages and ordinary people all come into the world the same way.

The path of death follows the design and development of the Lo-shu. From the Earlier Heaven of Ho-to emerges the Later Heaven of Lo-shu. From the Lo-shu, earth in the center dams up the water in the north and the kidneys are harmed. The water of the north puts out the fire of the south and the heart is harmed. The fire of the south melts the metal of the west and the lungs are injured. The metal of the west cuts down the wood the east and the liver is injured. The wood of the east chokes the earth in the center and the spleen is injured. When the five viscera are injured, the six bowels, and the hundred different parts of the body will all be harmed. Death and life are like ocean waves rolling one after the other. That is why it is said that being trapped in the cycle of rebirth and death is like sinking in the sea of suffering. Liquor, sex, riches, and anger are the four seas of suffering. If you do not wash away these seas of suffering, you will sink forever in them and lose the true way.

The sages say:

Know the secrets of the Ho-to and train early and diligently,
Return to the Origin and regain the One.
Escape from the net of the Lo-shu,
And your life will last longer than the Southern Mountains.

Persuade people to cultivate stillness and not be lazy,
Is there any reason why you should drown forever in the sea of suffering?

A hundred years of riches are but a flash of lightning,
When you have achieved the ultimate Breath you will have no worries.

Lao-tzu's book *Cultivating Stillness* delivers people from suffering,
It points out the sun, moon, and stars in the body,
Choosing between life and death is your own doing,
Buddhas and immortals are in your original spirit.

24

TRANSCENDENCE

超脫圖

超脫品二十四

法身

純陽仙象

純空無色

超脫

陰陽人象

空色相合

身

人

沈淪

純陰鬼象

空色俱無

死尸

If you can see intuitively, you will live the true and natural way. If you understand the Tao intuitively, you will always be pure and still.

Commentary

The Tao is wu-chi. The natural way is the great way of heaven. The three thousand and six hundred digressions are not the True Way. The True Way fosters a virtuous and upright mind. The false ways lead to hidden and secretive actions. Those who intuitively understand the Tao are those who understand the principles of life and original nature. They visit enlightened teachers who guide them in the ways of cultivating life and original mind. They are ready to receive the Tao and return to the Origin.

Intuitive understanding involves action, not just pure thinking. It is said that Bodhidharma arrived from the west and without a word bent his will to achieve enlightenment. The ancient sages say that no matter how intelligent you are, if you search for enlightenment through books and writings and do not have guidance from an enlightened teacher, you should not try the methods of training on your own. Those who intuitively understand the Tao are people who have accumulated good deeds. When the teacher appears, they must humbly ask the teacher for guidance. They must practice diligently and must not abandon their traning along the way. When the training is complete, they will be summoned and they will lose their shell and ascend to heaven. This is the sequence of searching for the Tao, asking for the Tao, receiving the Tao, understanding the Tao, cultivating the Tao, keeping the Tao, completing the Tao, and fulfilling the Tao. If you can accomplish these eight stages of attaining the Tao, then you will have accomplished your goal.

Being always pure and still means that you are forever at peace. Your original mind shines as brightly as the moon. Your deeds are done, your fruits are ripe, and you are filled with yang. The immortal children will lead you to ascend to the Nine Palaces. You will meet the buddhas and immortals at the capital of the Jade Emperor. You will be in the company of many ancestors and you will prostrate yourself before the Golden Mother. Your earthly deeds will be evaluated and you will be rewarded. According to the completeness of your fruit you will be given the title of Heavenly Lord Immortal. Your body will be covered with magnificent robes. Your stomach will be filled with the nectar of the immortals. According to the number of good deeds you have accumulated you will be given a place in one of the eight domains ruled by the Five Immortals. Depending on how your fruit ripens, you might be granted the right to live in the Central Heaven, or the Western Lands, both paradises of happiness. Or you may live in the thirty-six heavenly realms or the seventy-two earthly realms. Or you may live in the Three Pure Realms or the Ten Lands. All will be rewarded with justice according to their level of cultivation. In this way you will not have wasted your time on earth and the karma of being born human. You will be truly an honorable person above others existing in purity and stillness.

The sages say:

The teachings presented in *Cultivating Stillness*
Are suitable for men and women, young and old alike.
When the golden metal and the jade stone merge as one substance,
Ch'ien and k'un will ascend to the highest realm of heaven.

Hurry and find the center of true stillness,
Tame your mind and recover your original nature,
Distance yourself from the east and return to the west,
Gather the herbs and complete the alchemical transformation of the pill,
Let your body shed its mortal shell and ascend to the realm of heaven.

The book *Cultivating Stillness* and its associated illustrations
Are a raft that carries us across the sea of suffering,
The text helps to see through the illusion of life and death,
The commentary is a shaft of light through the dark well of ignorance.

The book *Cultivating Stillness* is both mysterious and wonderful,
We are grateful to the lords of heaven for revealing it to us.
Those who can penetrate the principles hidden in the text
Will inherit the treasures of the three religions.

Books by Eva Wong

Cultivating Stillness

Cultivating the Energy of Life

Feng-shui

Harmonizing Yin and Yang

Holding Yin, Embracing Yang

Lieh-tzu

A Master Course in Feng-shui

Nourishing the Essence of Life

Pocket Tao Reader

Seven Taoist Masters

The Shambhala Guide to Taoism

Tales of the Dancing Dragon

Tales of the Taoist Immortals

Teachings of the Tao